Copyright © 2020 by Isabelle Lapsley - All rights reserved.

The content contained within this book may not be reproduced, duplicated, or transmitted without direct written permission from the author or the publisher.Under no circumstances will any blame or legal responsibility be held against the publisher, or author, for any damages, reparation, or monetary loss due to the information contained within this book, either directly or indirectly.This book is copyright protected. It is only for personal use. You cannot amend, distribute, sell, use, quote or paraphrase any part, or the content within this book, without the consent of the author or publisher.

Please note the information contained within this document is for educational and entertainment purposes only. All effort has been executed to present accurate, up to date, reliable, complete information. No warranties of any kind are declared or implied. Readers acknowledge that the author is not engaged in the rendering of legal, financial, medical, or professional advice. The content within this book has been derived from various sources. Please consult a licensed professional before attempting any techniques outlined in this book.

By reading this document, the reader agrees that under no circumstances is the author responsible for any losses, direct or indirect, that are incurred as a result of the use of the information contained within this document, including, but not limited to, errors, omissions, or inaccuracies.

CONTENTS

INTRODUCTION 5
    What is the George Foreman Indoor Grill? 5
    What is the Pros and Cons? 5

VEGETARIAN RECIPES 7
    1. Pineapple & Veggie Skewers 7
    2. Haloumi Kebobs 8
    3. Buttered Corn 9
    4. Vinegar Veggies 10
    5. Goat Cheese & Tomato Stuffed Zucchini 11
    6. Grilled Tofu With Pineapple 12
    7. Guacamole 13
    8. Marinated Veggie Skewers 14
    9. Garlicky Mixed Veggies 15
    10. Mediterranean Veggies 16
    11. Caprese Eggplant Boats 17
    12. Grilled Pizza Margarita 18

BREAKFAST RECIPES 19
    13. Quick Oat & Banana Pancakes 19
    14. Classic Bacon And Eggs Breakfast 20
    15. Grilled Ham Omelet 21
    16. Corn Cakes With Salsa And Cream Cheese 22
    17. Sausage And Mushroom Breakfast Skewers 23
    18. Mexican Eggs On Haystacks 24
    19. Chocolate Chip And Blueberry Pancakes 25

APPETIZER & SIDE DISHES 26
    20. Sriracha Wings 26
    21. Brussel Sprout Skewers 27
    22. Balsamic Bell Peppers 28
    23. Simple Mushrooms 29
    24. Cauliflower Steaks 30
    25. Charred Tofu 31
    26. Grilled And Dressed Romaine Head 32
    27. Grilled Mushroom Skewers 33
    28. Lemony Green Beans 34
    29. Jalapeño Poppers 35
    30. Shrimp With Dipping Sauce 36
    31. Parmesan Zucchini 37

POULTRY RECIPES 38
    32. Chicken Burgers 38

33. Chicken Yakitori 39
34. Grilled Honey Chicken 40
35. Lemon And Rosemary Turkey And Zucchini Threads 41
36. Simple Cajun Chicken Legs 42
37. Peach Glazed Chicken Breasts 43
38. Tequila Chicken 44
39. Teriyaki Chicken Thighs 45
40. Chicken Drumsticks 46
41. Thyme Duck Breasts 47
42. Glazed Chicken Drumsticks 48
43. Lemon Grilled Chicken Thighs 49
44. Grilled Chicken Breast 50

FISH & SEAFOOD RECIPES 51
45. Orange-glazed Salmon 51
46. Seasoned Tuna 52
47. Lemon Pepper Salmon With Cherry Tomatoes And Asparagus 53
48. Lemon-garlic Salmon 54
49. The Easiest Pesto Shrimp 55
50. Barbecue Squid 56
51. Herbed Salmon 57
52. Ginger Salmon 58
53. Pistachio Pesto Shrimp 59
54. Grilled Garlic Scallops 60
55. Lemony Cod 61
56. Lemony Salmon 62

BEEF, PORK & LAMB RECIPES 63
57. American Burger 63
58. Fajita Skewers 64
59. Garlicky Flank Steak 65
60. Lamb Steak 66
61. Steak Skewers With Potatoes And Mushrooms 67
62. Cheese Burgers 68
63. Grilled Lamb With Herbes De Provence 69
64. Pork Kabobs 70
65. Grilled Pork Chops 71
66. Spiced Pork Tenderloin 72
67. Maple Pork Chops 73
68. Honey Glazed Pork Chops 74

BREADS AND SANDWICHES 75
69. The Greatest Butter Burger Recipe 75

70. Simple Pork Chop Sandwich ... 76
71. Chicken Pesto Grilled Sandwich ... 77
72. Fish Tacos With Slaw And Mango Salsa ... 78
73. Buttery Pepperoni Grilled Cheese Sandwich ... 79
74. Cheesy Buffalo Avocado Sandwich ... 80

SNACK & DESSERT RECIPES ... 81
75. Rum-soaked Pineapple ... 81
76. Fruit Kabobs ... 82
77. Grilled Apples ... 83
78. Cinnamon Sugar Grilled Apricots ... 84
79. Banana Butter Kabobs ... 85
80. Marshmallow Stuffed Banana ... 86
81. Peanut Butter Pancakes ... 87
82. Zucchini Rollups With Hummus ... 88
83. Coconut-coated Pineapple ... 89
84. Red Velvet Pancakes ... 90
85. Fruity Skewers ... 91
86. Blueberry Waffles ... 92

OTHER FAVORITE RECIPES ... 93
87. Pork And Veggie Salad ... 93
88. Shrimp Salad With Sour Cream And Dijon ... 94
89. Lamb Burgers ... 95
90. Scrambled Eggs And Cheese ... 96
91. Chocolate Panini ... 97
92. Beef Burgers ... 98
93. Turkey Burgers ... 99
94. Breakfast Panini ... 100
95. Grilled Watermelon Salad With Cucumber And Cheese ... 101
96. Stuffed Burgers ... 102
97. Sausage Scrambled Eggs ... 103
98. Grilled Zucchini And Feta Salad ... 104
99. Mexican Scrambled Eggs ... 105
100. Greek Grilled Salmon Salad ... 106

INTRODUCTION

What is the George Foreman Indoor Grill?

George Foreman was keen to make sure that buyers get value for their money with this grill. First and foremost, the grill can be used both indoors and outdoors due to its portable nature. Secondly, it cooks tasty dishes irrespective of the environment and the type of food you are preparing. Thirdly, the sloped coking surface clears grease residue from your culinary creation so that the final product is tasty and healthy. The smokeless indoor electric grill is an excellent choice for anyone who wants to prepare food at a moderate temperature for a lengthy period. It is ideal for tailgaters, families, and barbecue fanatics. The grilling surface is enough to cook up to fifteen servings of guests or family gatherings.

What is the Pros and Cons?

Pros
The cooking area is sloppy, to drain grease efficiently.
The domed hood helps develop convection currents that help with even cooking
Non-stick exterior keeps food cooking without burning
Removable grills for easy cleaning
Large enough to serve up to 15 people
Cons
The support clips are not durable enough
Irregular heating can undercook or overcook food

Things to consider when buying a George Foreman Indoor Grill
When deciding on the best indoor grill, you may need to consider things like its features and benefits. You must remember that not all grills work in the same way. So you should look for several features that suit your needs. You can start by thinking about these features before you invest in any of them. You can also take a look at the reviews of grills.

Switching on/off
You can check if your grill is equipped with a switch. It is helpful to obtain models that have a switch instead of a direct socket. Models that do not use a switch present a higher fire risk.

Temperature control
When it comes to cooking, it is important to consider how high the temperature can be. A typical grill should be designed for cooking meat with up to 1500 watts of power. It should be able to burn or brown meat. Cooking at low temperatures can cause meat to lose the desired texture.

Removable wire mesh panels
Removable plates can make cleaning easier. It is best to cook the meat raw. With this in mind, choose a grill with removable plates so that you do not have problems with cleaning and maintenance.

Cleaning procedure
It is important to find a smoke-free grill that is easy to clean after use. Many brands offer non-stick surfaces that prevent spills and hard-to-remove stains from sticking to the grill. In addition, easy-to-clean grills save you time that you can use for other important activities.

Kitchen area
Most indoor grills do not have much room to cook. However, you must choose a size that is large enough for the number of people you are cooking for. There are also models that allow you to cook different foods at the same time.

Tips and Tricks for Your George Foreman Indoor Grill
1. Turn off your grill and unplug it. If it's been in use, allow it to cool for at least 15 minutes.
2. Remove the grill plates and scrape off any loose scraps.
3. How do the plates look? If particularly grubby or burnt, put them in a sink or bowl filled with warm water and a few drops of washing-up liquid. Ten minutes should be long enough.
4. If you have a dishwasher, they can go straight in there (a regular wash programme and detergent is fine, just don't overload the washer to give the plates the best chance of getting clean).
5. Hand washing is straightforward: just use warm water and washing-up liquid. Give them a good clean with a sponge. Do not ever use a scouring pad or anything metallic as that risks stripping off the non-stick coating.
6. Ensure the plates are fully dry before putting them back so as to prevent any excess water short-circuiting the grill.

Your George Foreman grill cleaning questions answered
What is the easiest way to clean a George Foreman grill?
It depends on whether your grill has removable plates and how dirty it is. A simple wipe over with a soft, damp cloth might be enough, but if you're dealing with grime and stubborn residue then you'll need to use one of our methods above.

How do I get burnt food off my George Foreman grill?
Try the cleaning methods that we have outlined above. If you still have burnt bits that won't budge then try the chopstick trick: simply wrap the square end of a chopstick in a soft cloth and use it to work on the stuck bits. Failing that, crack open the baking soda, and sprinkle it on both sides of the grill. Place enough damp paper towels to fully cover the plates and then leave overnight. You should find the leftovers come easily unstuck.

Can you use oven cleaner on a George Foreman grill?
You want to be careful using any harsh chemicals on the non-stick plates as you could strip them of their coating, ruining them. While some milder cleaners may be fine, it's safer to use one of the methods above. In any case, check the manufacturer's instructions to make sure you won't cause any damage or invalidate a warranty. Are you looking to clean an outdoor grill? Follow our step-by-step guide on how to clean a BBQ, or check our advice on how to clean a gas barbecue.

VEGETARIAN RECIPES

1. Pineapple & Veggie Skewers

Servings: 6
Cooking Time: 15 Minutes

Ingredients:
- 1/3 cup olive oil
- 1½ teaspoons dried basil
- ¾ teaspoon dried oregano
- Salt and ground black pepper, as required
- 2 zucchinis, cut into 1-inch slices
- 2 yellow squash, cut into 1-inch slices
- ½ pound whole fresh mushrooms
- 1 red bell pepper, cut into chunks
- 1 red onion, cut into chunks
- 12 cherry tomatoes
- 1 fresh pineapple, cut into chunks

Directions:
1. In a bowl, add oil, herbs, salt ad black pepper and mix well.
2. Thread the veggies and pineapple onto pre-soaked wooden skewers.
3. Brush the veggiesand pineapple with oil mixture evenly.
4. Place the water tray in the bottom of George Foreman Grill .
5. Place about 2 cups of lukewarm water into the water tray.
6. Place the drip pan over water tray and then arrange the heating element.
7. Now, place the grilling pan over heating element.
8. Plugin the George Foreman Grill and press the 'Power' button to turn it on.
9. Then press 'Fan" button.
10. Set the temperature settings according to manufacturer's directions.
11. Cover the grill with lid and let it preheat.
12. After preheating, remove the lid and grease the grilling pan.
13. Place the skewers over the grilling pan.
14. Cover with the lid and cook for about 10-15 minutes, flipping occasionally.
15. Serve hot.

Nutrition Info: (Per Serving):Calories 220 ;Total Fat 11.9 g ;Saturated Fat 1.7 g ;Cholesterol 0 mg ;Sodium 47 mg ;Total Carbs 30 g ;Fiber 5 g ;Sugar 20.4 g ;Protein 4.3 g

2. Haloumi Kebobs

Servings: 4
Cooking Time: 5 Minutes

Ingredients:
- ½ pound Haloumi Cheese
- 4 Cremini Mushrooms, cut in half
- 1 Zucchini, cut into chunks
- ½ Bell Pepper, cut into chunks
- 2 tbsp Olive Oil
- Salt and Pepper, to taste

Directions:
1. Preheat your grill to 375 degrees F.
2. Meanwhile, soak 8 wooden skewers in water to preven burning.
3. Cut the cheese int chunks.
4. Thread the cheese and veggies onto the skewers, drizzle with the olive oil and sprinkle with salt and pepper.
5. Arrange onto the bottom plate, lower the lid, and cook closed for about 5 minutes (or more if you want it well-done).
6. Serve as desired and enjoy!

Nutrition Info: Calories 220 ;Total Fats 14g ;Carbs 6g ;Protein 5g ;Fiber: 1.2g

3. Buttered Corn

Servings: 6
Cooking Time: 20 Minutes

Ingredients:
- 6 fresh whole corn on the cob
- ½ cup butter, melted
- Salt, as required

Directions:
1. Husk the corn and remove all the silk.
2. Brush each corn with melted butter and sprinkle with salt.
3. Place the water tray in the bottom of George Foreman Grill .
4. Place about 2 cups of lukewarm water into the water tray.
5. Place the drip pan over water tray and then arrange the heating element.
6. Now, place the grilling pan over heating element.
7. Plugin the George Foreman Grill and press the 'Power' button to turn it on.
8. Then press 'Fan" button.
9. Set the temperature settings according to manufacturer's directions.
10. Cover the grill with lid and let it preheat.
11. After preheating, remove the lid and grease the grilling pan.
12. Place the corn over the grilling pan.
13. Cover with the lid and cook for about 20 minutes, rotating after every 5 minutes and brushing with butter once halfway through.
14. Serve warm.

Nutrition Info: (Per Serving):Calories 268 ;Total Fat 17.2 g ;Saturated Fat 10 g ;Cholesterol 41 mg ;Sodium 159 mg ;Total Carbs 29 g ;Fiber 4.2 g ;Sugar 5 g ;Protein 5.2 g

4. Vinegar Veggies

Servings: 4
Cooking Time: 10 Minutes

Ingredients:
- 3 golden beets, trimmed, peeled and sliced thinly
- 3 carrots, peeled and sliced lengthwise
- 1 cup zucchini, sliced
- 1 onion, sliced
- ½ cup yam, sliced thinly
- 2 tablespoon fresh rosemary
- 1 garlic clove, minced
- Salt and ground black pepper, as required
- 3 tablespoons vegetable oil
- 2 teaspoons balsamic vinegar

Directions:
1. Place all ingredients in a bowl and toss to coat well.
2. Refrigerate to marinate for at least 30 minutes.
3. Place the water tray in the bottom of George Foreman Grill .
4. Place about 2 cups of lukewarm water into the water tray.
5. Place the drip pan over water tray and then arrange the heating element.
6. Now, place the grilling pan over heating element.
7. Plugin the George Foreman Grill and press the 'Power' button to turn it on.
8. Then press 'Fan" button.
9. Set the temperature settings according to manufacturer's directions.
10. Cover the grill with lid and let it preheat.
11. After preheating, remove the lid and grease the grilling pan.
12. Place the vegetables over the grilling pan.
13. Cover with the lid and cook for about 5 minutes per side.
14. Serve hot.

Nutrition Info: (Per Serving):Calories 184 ;Total Fat 10.7 g ;Saturated Fat 2.2 g ;Cholesterol 0 mg ;Sodium 134 mg ;Total Carbs 21.5 g ;Fiber 4.9 g ;Sugar 10 g ;Protein 2.7 g

5. Goat Cheese & Tomato Stuffed Zucchini

Servings: 8
Cooking Time: 8 Minutes

Ingredients:
- 14 ounces Goat Cheese
- 1 ½ cups Tomato Sauce
- 4 medium Zucchini

Directions:
1. Preheat your grill to medium-high.
2. Cut the zucchini in half and scoop the seeds out.
3. Coat the grill with cooking spray and add the zucchini to it.
4. Lower the lid and cook for 2 minutes.
5. Now, add half of the goat cheese first, top with tomato sauce, and place the remaining cheese on top. Place a piece of aluminum foil on top of the filling so you don't make a big mess.
6. Carefully lower the grill and cook for an additional minute.
7. Serve and enjoy!

Nutrition Info: Calories 170 ;Total Fats 11g ;Carbs 8.2g ;Protein 10.5g ;Fiber: 2.3g

6. Grilled Tofu With Pineapple

Servings: 4
Cooking Time: 8 Minutes

Ingredients:
- 1 pound firm Tofu
- 1 Red Bell Pepper
- 1 Yello Bell Pepper
- 1 Zucchini
- ½ Pineapple
- ½ tsp Ginger Paste
- Salt and Pepper, to taste
- 2 tbsp Olive Oil

Directions:
1. Preheat your grill to medium-high.
2. Meanwhile, chop the tofu and vegies into smaller chunks, and place in a bowl. If using wooden skewers, soak them into water before using.
3. Add ginger and oil to the bowl and mix until coated well.
4. Thread the veggies and tofu onto the skewers.
5. When the green light turns on, open the grill and arrange the skewers onto the bottom plate.
6. Cook for 4 minutes, then flip over and cook for additional four minutes.
7. Serve as desired and enjoy!

Nutrition Info: Calories 210 ;Total Fats 12g ;Carbs 9g ;Protein 12g ;Fiber: 2g

7. Guacamole

Servings: 4
Cooking Time: 4 Minutes

Ingredients:
- 2 ripe avocados, halved and pitted
- 2 teaspoons vegetable oil
- 3 tablespoons fresh lime juice
- 1 garlic clove, crushed
- ¼ teaspoon ground chipotle chile
- Salt, as required
- ¼ cup red onion, chopped finely
- ¼ cup fresh cilantro, chopped finely

Directions:
1. Brush the cut sides of each avocado half with oil.
2. Place the water tray in the bottom of George Foreman Grill.
3. Place about 2 cups of lukewarm water into the water tray.
4. Place the drip pan over water tray and then arrange the heating element.
5. Now, place the grilling pan over heating element.
6. Plugin the George Foreman Grill and press the 'Power' button to turn it on.
7. Then press 'Fan" button.
8. Set the temperature settings according to manufacturer's directions.
9. Cover the grill with lid and let it preheat.
10. After preheating, remove the lid and grease the grilling pan.
11. Place the avocado halves over the grilling pan, cut side down.
12. Cook, uncovered for about 2-4 minutes.
13. Transfer the avocados onto cutting board and let them cool slightly.
14. Remove the peel and transfer the flesh into a bowl.
15. Add the lime juice, garlic, chipotle and salt and with a fork, mash until almost smooth.
16. Stir in onion and cilantro and refrigerate, covered for about 1 hour before serving.

Nutrition Info: (Per Serving):Calories 230 ;Total Fat 21.9 g ;Saturated Fat 4.6g ;Cholesterol 0 mg ;Sodium 46 mg ;Total Carbs 9.7 g ;Fiber 6.9 g ;Sugar 0.8 g ;Protein 2.1 g

8. Marinated Veggie Skewers

Servings: 4
Cooking Time: 10 Minutes

Ingredients:
- For Marinade:
- 2 garlic cloves, minced
- 2 teaspoons fresh basil, minced
- 2 teaspoons fresh oregano, minced
- ½ teaspoon cayenne pepper
- Sea Salt and ground black pepper, as required
- 2 tablespoons fresh lemon juice
- 2 tablespoons olive oil
- For Veggies:
- 2 large zucchinis, cut into thick slices
- 8 large button mushrooms, quartered
- 1 yellow bell pepper, seeded and cubed
- 1 red bell pepper, seeded and cubed

Directions:
1. For marinade: in a large bowl, add all the ingredients and mix until well combined.
2. Add the vegetables and toss to coat well.
3. Cover and refrigerate to marinate for at least 6-8 hours.
4. Remove the vegetables from the bowl and thread onto pre-soaked wooden skewers.
5. Place the water tray in the bottom of George Foreman Grill.
6. Place about 2 cups of lukewarm water into the water tray.
7. Place the drip pan over water tray and then arrange the heating element.
8. Now, place the grilling pan over heating element.
9. Plugin the George Foreman Grill and press the 'Power' button to turn it on.
10. Then press 'Fan" button.
11. Set the temperature settings according to manufacturer's directions.
12. Cover the grill with lid and let it preheat.
13. After preheating, remove the lid and grease the grilling pan.
14. Place the skewers over the grilling pan.
15. Cover with the lid and cook for about 8-10 minutes, flipping occasionally.
16. Serve hot.

Nutrition Info: (Per Serving):Calories 122 ;Total Fat 7.8 g ;Saturated Fat 1.2 g ;Cholesterol 0 mg ;Sodium 81 mg ;Total Carbs 12.7 g ;Fiber 3.5 g ;Sugar 6.8g ;Protein 4.3 g

9. Garlicky Mixed Veggies

Servings: 4
Cooking Time: 8 Minutes

Ingredients:
- 1 bunch fresh asparagus, trimmed
- 6 ounces fresh mushrooms, halved
- 6 Campari tomatoes, halved
- 1 red onion, cut into 1-inch chunks
- 3 garlic cloves, minced
- 2 tablespoons olive oil
- Salt and ground black pepper, as required

Directions:
1. In a large bowl, add all ingredients and toss to coat well.
2. Place the water tray in the bottom of George Foreman Grill .
3. Place about 2 cups of lukewarm water into the water tray.
4. Place the drip pan over water tray and then arrange the heating element.
5. Now, place the grilling pan over heating element.
6. Plugin the George Foreman Grill and press the 'Power' button to turn it on.
7. Then press 'Fan" button.
8. Set the temperature settings according to manufacturer's directions.
9. Cover the grill with lid and let it preheat.
10. After preheating, remove the lid and grease the grilling pan.
11. Place the vegetables over the grilling pan.
12. Cover with the lid and cook for about 8 minutes, flipping occasionally.

Nutrition Info: (Per Serving):Calories 137 ;Total Fat 7.7 g ;Saturated Fat 1.1 g ;Cholesterol 0 mg ;Sodium 54 mg ;Total Carbs 15.6 g ;Fiber 5.6 g ;Sugar 8.9 g ;Protein 5.8 g

10. Mediterranean Veggies

Servings: 4
Cooking Time: 10 Minutes

Ingredients:
- 1 cup mixed bell peppers, chopped
- 1 cup eggplant, chopped
- 1 cup zucchini, chopped
- 1 cup mushrooms, chopped
- ½ cup onion, chopped
- ½ cup sun-dried tomato vinaigrette dressing

Directions:
1. In a large bowl, add all ingredients and toss to coat well.
2. Refrigerate to marinate for about 1 hour.
3. Place the water tray in the bottom of George Foreman Grill .
4. Place about 2 cups of lukewarm water into the water tray.
5. Place the drip pan over water tray and then arrange the heating element.
6. Now, place the grilling pan over heating element.
7. Plugin the George Foreman Grill and press the 'Power' button to turn it on.
8. Then press 'Fan" button.
9. Set the temperature settings according to manufacturer's directions.
10. Cover the grill with lid and let it preheat.
11. After preheating, remove the lid and grease the grilling pan.
12. Place the vegetables over the grilling pan.
13. Cover with the lid and cook for about 8-10 minutes, flipping occasionally.
14. Serve hot.

Nutrition Info: (Per Serving):Calories 159 ;Total Fat 11.2 g ;Saturated Fat 2 g ;Cholesterol 0 mg ;Sodium 336 mg ;Total Carbs 12.3 g ;Fiber 1.9 g ;Sugar 9.5 g ;Protein 1.6 g

11. Caprese Eggplant Boats

Servings: 4
Cooking Time: 10 Minutes

Ingredients:
- 2 Eggplants
- 1 cup Cherry Tomatoes, halved
- 1 cup Mozzarella Balls, chopped
- 2 tbsp Olive Oil
- 4 tbsp chopped Basil Leaves
- Salt and Pepper, to taste

Directions:
1. Preheat your grill to 375 degrees F.
2. Cut the eggplants in half (no need to peel them- just wash well), drizzle with olive oil and season with salt and pepper, generously.
3. When the green light is on, open the grill and arrange the eggplant halves onto the bottom plate.
4. Lower the lid and cook for about 4-5 minutes, until well-done.
5. Transfer to a serving plate and top with cherry tomatoes, mozzarella and basil.
6. Serve and enjoy!

Nutrition Info: Calories 187 ;Total Fats 11g ;Carbs 18.3g ;Protein 6.8g ;Fiber: 7.3g

12. Grilled Pizza Margarita

Servings: 1
Cooking Time: 2 Minutes

Ingredients:
- 1 Tortilla
- 3 tbsp Tomato Sauce
- 3 ounces shredded Mozzarella
- 4 Basil Leaves, chopped
- Pinch of Salt

Directions:
1. Preheat your grill to medium-high.
2. Unlock to lower the griddle and lay it on your counter.
3. When the green light turns on, add the tortilla to the grill, and lower the lid.
4. Cook only for about 40 seconds, just until it becomes hot.
5. Add the tomato sauce on top, sprinkle with cheese, basil, and some salt.
6. Cook for another minute or so – with the lid OFF – until the cheese becomes melted.
7. Serve and enjoy!

Nutrition Info: Calories 375 ;Total Fats 22g ;Carbs 23g ;Protein 22g ;Fiber: 2g

BREAKFAST RECIPES

13. Quick Oat & Banana Pancakes

Servings: 4
Cooking Time: 5 Minutes

Ingredients:
- ½ cup Oats
- ¼ cup chopped Nuts by choice (Walnuts and Hazelnuts work best)
- 1 large Ripe Banana, chopped finely
- 2 cups Pancake Mix

Directions:
1. Preheat your grill to medium and unlock the hinge. Open it flat on your counter.
2. Meanwhile, prepare the pancake mix according to the instruction on the package.
3. Stir in the remaining ingredients well.
4. Spray the griddle with some cooking spray.
5. Drop about ¼ cup onto the griddle.
6. Cook for a minute or two, just until the pancake begins to puff up.
7. Flip over and cook for another minute or so – the recipe makes about 16 pancakes.
8. Serve as desired and enjoy!

Nutrition Info: Calories 310 ;Total Fats 8g ;Carbs 56g ;Protein 14g ;Fiber: 8g

14. Classic Bacon And Eggs Breakfast

Servings: 1
Cooking Time: 8 Minutes

Ingredients:
- 2 Eggs
- 2 Bacon Slices
- 2 Bread Slices
- Salt and Pepper, to taste

Directions:
1. Preheat your grill to 400 degrees F, and make sure that the kickstand is in position.
2. When the light goes on, add the bacon to the plate and lower the lid.
3. Let cook for 4 full minutes.
4. Open the lid and crack the eggs onto the plate. Season with salt and pepper.
5. Add the bread slices to the plate, as well.
6. Cook for 4 minutes, turning the bread and bacon (and the eggs if you desire) over halfway through.
7. Transfer carefully to a plate. Enjoy!

Nutrition Info: Calories 434 ;Total Fats 19.6g ;Carbs 38.8g ;Protein 25.6g ;Fiber: 6g

15. Grilled Ham Omelet

Servings: 2
Cooking Time: 5 Minutes

Ingredients:
- 6 Eggs
- 2 Ham Slices, chopped
- 2 tbsp chopped Herbs by choice
- ¼ tsp Onion Powder
- 1 tbsp minced Red Pepper
- ¼ tsp Garlic Powder
- Salt and Pepper, to taste

Directions:
1. Preheat your grill to 350 degrees F.
2. In the meantime, whisk the eggs in a bowl and add the rest of the ingredients to it. Stir well to combine.
3. Open the grill and unlock the hinge.
4. Coat the griddle with some cooking spray and gently pour the egg mixture onto it.
5. With a silicone spatula, mix the omelet as you would in a skillet.
6. When it reaches your desired consistency, divide among two serving plates.
7. Enjoy!

Nutrition Info: Calories 271 ;Total Fats 17.5g ;Carbs 2.4g ;Protein 24g ;Fiber: 0.1g

16. Corn Cakes With Salsa And Cream Cheese

Servings: 8
Cooking Time: 8 Minutes

Ingredients:
- ½ cup Cornmeal
- ¼ cup Butter, melted
- ½ cup Salsa
- 14 ounces canned Corn, drained
- 1 cup Milk
- 6 ounces Cream Cheese
- 1 ½ cups Flour
- 6 Eggs
- ¼ cup chopped Spring Onions
- 1 tsp Baking Powder
- Salt and Pepper, to taste

Directions:
1. In a bowl, whisk together the eggs, butter, cream cheese, and milk.
2. Whisk in the cornmeal, flour, baking powder, salt, and pepper.
3. Fold in the remaining ingredients and stir well to incorporate.
4. Preheat your grill to medium.
5. When the light is on, unlock the hinge and lower to your counter.
6. Spray the griddle with a nonstick spray.
7. Ladle the batter onto the griddle (about ¼ of cup per cake).
8. When the cakes start bubbling, flip them over and cook until golden brown.
9. Serve as desired and enjoy!

Nutrition Info: Calories 325 ;Total Fats 15g ;Carbs 35g ;Protein 11g ;Fiber: 3g

17. Sausage And Mushroom Breakfast Skewers

Servings: 4
Cooking Time: 4 Minutes

Ingredients:
- 2 Italian Sausage Links
- 4 Whole White Button Mushrooms
- 1 Red Bell Pepper
- Salt and Pepper, to taste

Directions:
1. Soak four skewers in cold water for 2-3 minutes.
2. Preheat your grill to 375 degrees F.
3. Meanwhile, cut each sausage in eight pieces.
4. Quarter the mushrooms and cut the red pepper into eight pieces.
5. Sprinkle the mushrooms and pepper generously with salt and pepper.
6. Grab the skewers and thread the ingredients – sausage, mushroom, pepper, sausage, mushroom, sausage mushroom, pepper, sausage, mushroom, in that order.
7. Place onto the grill and lower the lid.
8. Cook for 4 minutes closed.
9. Serve alongside some bread and a favorite spread and enjoy.

Nutrition Info: Calories 118 ;Total Fats 9.1g ;Carbs 4g ;Protein 7.3g ;Fiber: 0.6g

18. Mexican Eggs On Haystacks

Servings: 6
Cooking Time: 12 Minutes

Ingredients:
- ½ cup Breadcrumbs
- 3 ½ cups Store-Bought Hash Browns
- 2/3 cup Sour Cream
- 2 tsp Tex Mex Seasoning
- 6 Eggs
- 1/3 cup shredded Cheddar
- Salt and Pepper, to taste

Directions:
1. Preheat your grill to medium.
2. In the meantime, squeeze the hash browns to get rid of excess water, and place in a bowl.
3. Add the breadcrumbs, cheese, half of the Tex-Mex, and season with some salt and pepper.
4. Mix with your hands to combine.
5. Open the grill, unlock the hinge for the griddle, and lay it open. Spray with cooking spray.
6. Make six patties out of the hash brown mixture and arrange onto the griddle.
7. Cook for 7 minutes, flipping once, halfway through. Tarsnsfer to six serving plates.
8. Crack the eggs open onto the griddle, season with salt and pepper, and cook until they reach your preferred consistency.
9. Top the hash browns with the egg.
10. Combine the sourcream and remaining Tex Mex and top the eggs with it.
11. Enjoy!

Nutrition Info: Calories 340 ;Total Fats 21g ;Carbs 25g ;Protein 8.2g ;Fiber: 2g

19. Chocolate Chip And Blueberry Pancakes

Servings: 2
Cooking Time: 5 Minutes

Ingredients:
- 1 cup Pancake Mix
- ¼ cup Orange Juice
- 1/3 cup Fresh Blueberries
- ¼ cup Chocolate Chips
- ½ cup Water

Directions:
1. Preheat your grill to medium.
2. Meanwhile, combine the pancake mix with the orange juice and water.
3. Fold in the chocolate chips and blueberries.
4. Open the grill, unhinge, and lay the griddle onto your counter.
5. Spray with cooking spray.
6. Add about 1/6 of the batter at a time, to the griddle.
7. Cook until bubbles start forming on the surface, then flip over, and cook until the other side turns golden brown.
8. Serve and enjoy!

Nutrition Info: Calories 370 ;Total Fats 9g ;Carbs 66g ;Protein 3g ;Fiber: 3g

APPETIZER & SIDE DISHES

20.   Sriracha Wings

Servings: 8
Cooking Time: 18 Minutes

Ingredients:
- For Wings:
- 3 pounds chicken wings
- 1 tablespoon canola oil
- 2 teaspoons ground coriander
- ½ teaspoon garlic salt
- ¼ teaspoon ground black pepper
- For Sauce:
- ½ cup fresh orange juice
- 1/3 cup Sriracha chili sauce
- ¼ cup butter, melted
- 3 tablespoons honey
- 2 tablespoons lime juice
- ¼ cup fresh cilantro, chopped

Directions:
1. For wings: in a bowl, place all ingredients and toss to coat well.
2. Cover the bowl and refrigerate for about 2 hours or overnight.
3. For sauce: in a bowl, place orange juice, chili sauce, butter, honey and lime juice and mix until well combined. Set aside.
4. Place the water tray in the bottom of George Foreman Grill .
5. Place about 2 cups of lukewarm water into the water tray.
6. Place the drip pan over water tray and then, arrange the heating element.
7. Now, place the grilling pan over heating element.
8. Plugin the George Foreman Grill and press the 'Power' button to turn it on.
9. Then press 'Fan" button.
10. Set the temperature settings according to manufacturer's directions.
11. Cover the grill with lid and let it preheat.
12. After preheating, remove the lid and grease the grilling pan.
13. Place the chicken wings over the grilling pan.
14. Cover with the lid and cook for about 15-18 minutes, flipping occasionally.
15. In the last 5 minutes of cooking, brush the wings with some of the sauce.
16. Transfer chicken into the bowl of the remaining sauce and toss to coat.
17. Garnish with cilantro and serve.

Nutrition Info: (Per Serving):Calories 432 ;Total Fat 20.1 g ;Saturated Fat 7.3 g ;Cholesterol 167 mg ;Sodium 258 mg ;Total Carbs 10.5 g ;Fiber 0.1 g ;Sugar 7.9 g ;Protein 49.5 g

21. Brussel Sprout Skewers

Servings: 8
Cooking Time: 7 Minutes

Ingredients:
- 24 Brussel Sprouts
- 2 tbsp Balsamic Glaze
- 4 tbsp Olive Oil
- ½ tsp Garlic Powder
- Salt and Pepper, to taste

Directions:
1. Preheat your grill to 375 degrees F.
2. In the meantime, trim the brussel sprouts and cut the in half.
3. Thread onto soaked wooden or metal skewers.
4. Drizzle with olive oil and sprinkle with the seasonings.
5. Place onto the bottom plate and cook uncovered for 4 minutes.
6. Turn over and cook for another 3 minutes or so.
7. Serve as desired and enjoy!

Nutrition Info: Calories 92 ;Total Fats 6g ;Carbs 6g ;Protein 1g ;Fiber: 2g

22. Balsamic Bell Peppers

Servings: 4
Cooking Time: 10 Minutes

Ingredients:
- 1 pound small bell peppers, halved and seeded
- 1 tablespoon olive oil
- Salt and ground black pepper, as required
- 1 tablespoon balsamic vinegar

Directions:
1. Brush the bell pepper halves with oil and then sprinkle with salt and pepper.
2. Place the water tray in the bottom of George Foreman Grill .
3. Place about 2 cups of lukewarm water into the water tray.
4. Place the drip pan over water tray and then arrange the heating element.
5. Now, place the grilling pan over heating element.
6. Plugin the George Foreman Grill and press the 'Power' button to turn it on.
7. Then press 'Fan" button.
8. Set the temperature settings according to manufacturer's directions.
9. Cover the grill with lid and let it preheat.
10. After preheating, remove the lid and grease the grilling pan.
11. Place the bell pepper halves over the grilling pan.
12. Cover with the lid and cook for about 8-10 minutes, flipping once halfway through.
13. Transfer the bell pepper halves onto a plate and drizzle with vinegar.
14. Serve immediately.

Nutrition Info: (Per Serving):Calories 40 ;Total Fat 3.6 g ;Saturated Fat 0.5 g ;Cholesterol 0mg ;Sodium 40 mg ;Total Carbs 2.3 g ;Fiber 0.4 g ;Sugar 1.5 g ;Protein 0.3 g

23. Simple Mushrooms

Servings: 2
Cooking Time: 5 Minutes

Ingredients:
- 8 ounces shiitake mushrooms, stems discarded
- 1 tablespoon vegetable oil
- 1 garlic clove, minced
- Salt and ground black pepper, as required

Directions:
1. In a bowl, place all ingredients and toss to coat well.
2. Place the water tray in the bottom of George Foreman Grill.
3. Place about 2 cups of lukewarm water into the water tray.
4. Place the drip pan over water tray and then arrange the heating element.
5. Now, place the grilling pan over heating element.
6. Plugin the George Foreman Grill and press the 'Power' button to turn it on.
7. Then press 'Fan" button.
8. Set the temperature settings according to manufacturer's directions.
9. Cover the grill with lid and let it preheat.
10. After preheating, remove the lid and grease the grilling pan.
11. Place the mushrooms over the grilling pan.
12. Cover with the lid and cook for about 4-5 minutes, turning occasionally.
13. Serve hot.

Nutrition Info: (Per Serving):Calories 87 ;Total Fat 7.1 g ;Saturated Fat 1.3 g ;Cholesterol 0 mg ;Sodium 84 mg ;Total Carbs 4.2 g ;Fiber 1.2 g ;Sugar 2 g ;Protein 3.7 g

24. Cauliflower Steaks

Servings: 4
Cooking Time: 9 Minutes

Ingredients:
- 2 large heads cauliflower
- ¼ cup olive oil
- ½ teaspoons garlic powder
- ½ teaspoons paprika
- Kosher salt, to taste
- Black pepper, to taste
- 2 cups cheddar cheese, shredded
- Ranch dressing, for drizzling
- 8 cooked bacon slices, crumbled
- 2 tablespoons chives, chopped

Directions:
1. Mix olive oil, garlic powder, paprika, salt, and black pepper in a bowl
2. Slice the cauliflower into ¾ inch thick steaks and rub them with the olive oil mixture.
3. Turn the "Selector" knob to the "Grill Panini" side.
4. Preheat the bottom grill of George Foreman Grill at 350 degrees F and the upper grill plate on medium heat.
5. Once it is preheated, open the lid and place the cauliflower steaks in the Griddler.
6. Close the griddler's lid and grill the steaks for 8 minutes until lightly charred.
7. Open the lid and drizzle bacon, cheddar cheese, ranch dressing and chives on top.
8. Cook for 1 minute until the cheese is melted.
9. Serve warm.

Nutrition Info: (Per Serving): Calories 278 ;Total Fat 3.8 g ;Saturated Fat 0.7 g ;Cholesterol 2 mg ;Sodium 620 mg ;Total Carbs 13.3 g ;Fiber 2.4 g ;Sugar 1.2 g ;Protein 5.4 g

25. Charred Tofu

Servings: 3
Cooking Time: 15 Minutes

Ingredients:
- 12 ounces extra-firm tofu, pressed, drained and cut into ½-inch thick slices
- Salt and ground black pepper, as required

Directions:
1. Season the tofu slices with salt and pepper.
2. Place the water tray in the bottom of George Foreman Grill .
3. Place about 2 cups of lukewarm water into the water tray.
4. Place the drip pan over water tray and then arrange the heating element.
5. Now, place the grilling pan over heating element.
6. Plugin the George Foreman Grill and press the 'Power' button to turn it on.
7. Then press 'Fan" button.
8. Set the temperature settings according to manufacturer's directions.
9. Cover the grill with lid and let it preheat.
10. After preheating, remove the lid and grease the grilling pan.
11. Place the mushrooms over the grilling pan.
12. Cover with the lid and cook for about 10-15 minutes, flipping once halfway through.
13. Serve warm.

Nutrition Info: (Per Serving):Calories 103 ;Total Fat 6.6 g ;Saturated Fat 0.6 g ;Cholesterol 0 mg ;Sodium 59 mg ;Total Carbs 2.3 g ;Fiber 0.5 g ;Sugar 0.6 g ;Protein 11.2 g

26. Grilled And Dressed Romaine Head

Servings: 4
Cooking Time: 5 Minutes

Ingredients:
- 2 Hearts of Romaine
- ½ cup Olive Oil
- 2 Eg Yolks
- 2 Whole Garlic Cloves
- ½ tsp Dijon Mustard
- 2 Anchovies
- 3 tbsp Parmesan Cheese
- 4 tbsp Lemon Juice
- Salt an Pepper, to taste

Directions:
1. Preheat your grill to medium high.
2. Place all of the dressing ingredients to the bowl of your food processor.
3. Pulse until smooth and set aside.
4. When the grill is ready, open the lid and spray with some cooking spray.
5. Place the romaine heart onto the bottom plate and cook for 3 minutes.
6. Flip over and cook for 2 more minutes.
7. Arrange on a large serving plate.
8. Drizzle with the dressing.
9. Enjoy!

Nutrition Info: Calories 88 ;Total Fats 4g ;Carbs 3g ;Protein 2.5g ;Fiber: 0.4g

27. Grilled Mushroom Skewers

Servings: 6
Cooking Time: 3 Minutes

Ingredients:
- 2 pounds mushrooms, sliced
- 2 tablespoons balsamic vinegar
- 1 tablespoon soy sauce
- 3 garlic cloves, chopped
- 1/2 teaspoon thyme, chopped
- Salt and black pepper to taste

Directions:
1. Toss mushrooms with balsamic vinegar, soy sauce, garlic, thyme, black pepper and salt in a bowl.
2. Thread the mushroom slices on mini wooden skewers.
3. Turn the "Selector" knob to the "Grill Panini" side.
4. Preheat the bottom grill of George Foreman Grill at 350 degrees F and the upper grill plate on medium heat.
5. Once it is preheated, open the lid and place mushroom skewers horizontally in the Griddler.
6. Close the griddler's lid and grill the mushrooms for 3 minutes.
7. Serve warm.

Nutrition Info: (Per Serving): Calories 418 ;Total Fat 15.7 g ;Saturated Fat 2.7 g ;Cholesterol 75 mg ;Sodium 94 mg ;Total Carbs 10.4 g ;Fiber 0.1 g ;Sugar 0.3 g ;Protein 4.9 g

28. Lemony Green Beans

Servings: 3
Cooking Time: 6 Minutes

Ingredients:
- 2 tablespoons canola oil
- 2 garlic cloves, crushed
- 1 teaspoon red chili powder
- Salt, as required
- 1 pound fresh asparagus, trimmed

Directions:
1. In a bowl, place all ingredients except for lemon juice and toss to coat well.
2. Place the water tray in the bottom of George Foreman Grill .
3. Place about 2 cups of lukewarm water into the water tray.
4. Place the drip pan over water tray and then arrange the heating element.
5. Now, place the grilling pan over heating element.
6. Plugin the George Foreman Grill and press the 'Power' button to turn it on.
7. Then press 'Fan" button.
8. Set the temperature settings according to manufacturer's directions.
9. Cover the grill with lid and let it preheat.
10. After preheating, remove the lid and grease the grilling pan.
11. Place the asparagus over the grilling pan.
12. Cover with the lid and cook for about 5-6 minutes, turning occasionally.
13. Transfer the green beans into a bowl and drizzle with lemon juice.
14. Serve hot.

Nutrition Info: (Per Serving):Calories 118 ;Total Fat 9.7 g ;Saturated Fat 0.8 g ;Cholesterol 0mg ;Sodium 63 mg ;Total Carbs 7 g ;Fiber 3.5 g ;Sugar 2.9 g ;Protein 3.6 g

29. Jalapeño Poppers

Servings: 12
Cooking Time: 30 Minutes

Ingredients:
- 24 medium jalapeño peppers
- 1 pound uncooked chorizo pork sausage, crumbled
- 2 cups cheddar cheese, shredded
- 12 bacon strips, cut in half

Directions:
1. Cut each jalapeno in half lengthwise, about 1/8-inch deep.
2. Then remove the seeds.
3. In a bowl, place the sausage and cheese and mix well.
4. Stuff the jalapeño peppers with cheese mixture and then wrap each with a piece of bacon.
5. With toothpicks, secure each jalapeño pepper.
6. Place the water tray in the bottom of George Foreman Grill.
7. Place about 2 cups of lukewarm water into the water tray.
8. Place the drip pan over water tray and then, arrange the heating element.
9. Now, place the grilling pan over heating element.
10. Plugin the George Foreman Grill and press the 'Power' button to turn it on.
11. Then press 'Fan" button.
12. Set the temperature settings according to manufacturer's directions.
13. Cover the grill with lid and let it preheat.
14. After preheating, remove the lid and grease the grilling pan.
15. Place the jalapeño peppers over the grilling pan.
16. Cover with the lid and cook for about 35-40 minutes, flipping once halfway through.
17. Discard the toothpicks and serve warm.

Nutrition Info: (Per Serving):Calories 373 ;Total Fat 29.5 g ;Saturated Fat 11.4 g ;Cholesterol 83 mg ;Sodium 1800 mg ;Total Carbs 2.7 g ;Fiber 1.1 g ;Sugar 1 g ;Protein 23.2 g

30. Shrimp With Dipping Sauce

Servings: 6
Cooking Time: 4 Minutes

Ingredients:
- 1½ pounds jumbo shrimp, peeled, deveined, and patted dry
- 2 teaspoons canola oil
- ¼ teaspoon paprika
- Salt and ground black pepper, as required
- ¼ cup warm jalapeño jelly
- ¼ cup chili sauce

Directions:
1. Brush the shrimp with oil lightly and then sprinkle with paprika, salt and black pepper.
2. Place the water tray in the bottom of George Foreman Grill.
3. Place about 2 cups of lukewarm water into the water tray.
4. Place the drip pan over water tray and then, arrange the heating element.
5. Now, place the grilling pan over heating element.
6. Plugin the George Foreman Grill and press the 'Power' button to turn it on.
7. Then press 'Fan" button.
8. Set the temperature settings according to manufacturer's directions.
9. Cover the grill with lid and let it preheat.
10. After preheating, remove the lid and grease the grilling pan.
11. Place the shrimp over the grilling pan.
12. Cover with the lid and cook for about 2 minutes per side.
13. Meanwhile, in a bowl, place jalapeño jelly and chili sauce and mix well.
14. Serve warm shrimp with dipping sauce.

Nutrition Info: (Per Serving):Calories 167 ;Total Fat 3.5 g ;Saturated Fat 0.7 g ;Cholesterol 239 mg ;Sodium 584 mg ;Total Carbs 6.6 g ;Fiber 0.1 g ;Sugar 4.1 g ;Protein 25.9 g

31. Parmesan Zucchini

Servings: 4
Cooking Time: 7 Minutes

Ingredients:
- 3 medium zucchinis, cut into ½-inch slices
- 2 tablespoons extra-virgin olive oil
- Salt and ground black pepper, as required
- ¼ cup parmesan cheese, shredded

Directions:
1. Brush the zucchini slices with oil and then sprinkle with salt and pepper.
2. Place the water tray in the bottom of George Foreman Grill .
3. Place about 2 cups of lukewarm water into the water tray.
4. Place the drip pan over water tray and then arrange the heating element.
5. Now, place the grilling pan over heating element.
6. Plugin the George Foreman Grill and press the 'Power' button to turn it on.
7. Then press 'Fan" button.
8. Set the temperature settings according to manufacturer's directions.
9. Cover the grill with lid and let it preheat.
10. After preheating, remove the lid and grease the grilling pan.
11. Place the zucchini slices over the grilling pan.
12. Cover with the lid and cook for about 5-7 minutes, flipping once halfway through.
13. Transfer the zucchini slices onto a plate and sprinkle with cheese.
14. Serve immediately.

Nutrition Info: (Per Serving):Calories 104 ;Total Fat 8.6 g ;Saturated Fat 1.9 g ;Cholesterol 4 mg ;Sodium 138 mg ;Total Carbs 5.1 g ;Fiber 1.6 g ;Sugar 2.5 g ;Protein 3.7 g

POULTRY RECIPES

32. Chicken Burgers

Servings: 5
Cooking Time: 6 Minutes

Ingredients:
- 1 tablespoon butter, melted
- 1 small red onion, chopped
- 2 garlic cloves, chopped
- 2 tablespoons tomato paste
- 1 teaspoon sugar
- 1 tablespoon Worcestershire sauce
- 1 tablespoon hot sauce
- 1 1/4 pounds ground chicken
- 3 tablespoons olive oil
- 2 tablespoons honey

Directions:
1. Mix onion, butter, garlic, ground chicken, olive oil, honey, Worcestershire sauce, and sugar in a bowl.
2. Make the chicken patties out of this mixture.
3. Turn the "Selector" knob to the "Grill Panini" side.
4. Preheat the bottom grill of George Foreman Grill at 350 degrees F and the upper grill plate on medium heat.
5. Once it is preheated, open the lid and place the patties in the Griddler.
6. Close the griddler's lid and grill the patties for 6 minutes.
7. Serve warm.

Nutrition Info: (Per Serving): Calories 529 ;Total Fat 17 g ;Saturated Fat 3 g ;Cholesterol 65 mg ;Sodium 391 mg ;Total Carbs 55 g ;Fiber 6 g ;Sugar 8 g ;Protein 41g

33. Chicken Yakitori

Servings: 4
Cooking Time: 6 Minutes

Ingredients:
- 2 tbsp Honey
- 1 tsp minced Garlic
- 1-pound boneless Chicken
- 1 tsp minced Ginger
- 4 tbsp Soy Sauce
- Salt and Pepper, to taste

Directions:
1. In a bowl, combine the honey, ginger, soy sauce, and garlic. Add some salt and pepper.
2. Cut the chicken into thick stripes and add them to the bowl.
3. Mix until the meat is completely coated with the marinade.
4. Cover the bowl and refrigerate for about one hour.
5. Preheat your grill to medium.
6. Thread the chicken onto metal (or soaked wooden) skewers and arrange onto the bottom plate.
7. Lower the lid and cook for about 6-7 minutes, depending on how well-cooked you prefer the meat to be.
8. Serve and enjoy!

Nutrition Info: Calories 182 ;Total Fats 9g ;Carbs 10g ;Protein 27g ;Fiber: 0.2g

34. Grilled Honey Chicken

Servings: 4
Cooking Time: 6 Minutes

Ingredients:
- Juice of 2 lemons
- ½ tablespoon Dijon mustard
- 1 tablespoon honey
- A dash of salt
- 2 whole chicken breasts

Directions:
1. Rub the chicken with honey, salt, Dijon and lemon juice.
2. Turn the "Selector" knob to the "Grill Panini" side.
3. Preheat the bottom grill of George Foreman Grill at 350 degrees F and the upper grill plate on medium heat.
4. Once it is preheated, open the lid and place the chicken breasts in the Griddler.
5. Close the griddler's lid and grill the chicken for 6 minutes.
6. Serve warm.

Nutrition Info: (Per Serving): Calories 231 ;Total Fat 20.1 g ;Saturated Fat 2.4 g ;Cholesterol 110 mg ;Sodium 941 mg ;Total Carbs 30.1 g ;Fiber 0.9 g ;Sugar 1.4 g ;Protein 14.6 g

35. Lemon And Rosemary Turkey And Zucchini Threads

Servings: 4
Cooking Time: 7 Minutes

Ingredients:
- 1-pound Turkey Breasts, boneless and skinless
- 1 Large Zuchinni
- 2 tbsp Lemon Juice
- ½ tsp Lemon Zest
- ¼ cup Olive Oil
- 1 tbsp Honey
- 1 tbsp Fresh Rosemary
- ¼ tsp Garlic Powder
- Salt and Pepper, to taste

Directions:
1. Cut the Turkey into smaller chunks, and place inside a bowl.
2. Add the olive oil, lemon juice, zest, honey, rosemary, garlic powder, and some salt and pepper, to the bowl.
3. With your hands, mix well until the turkey is completely coated with the mixture.
4. Cover and let sit in the fridge for about an hour.
5. Wash the zucchini thoroughly and cut into small chunks. Season with salt and pepper.
6. Preheat your Grill to 350 – 375 degrees F.
7. Thread the turkey and zucchini onto soaked (or metal) skewers and arrange on the bottom plate.
8. Lower the lid and cook closed for 6-7 minutes.
9. Serve and enjoy!

Nutrition Info: Calories 280 ;Total Fats 23g ;Carbs 6g ;Protein 27g ;Fiber: 0.5g

36. Simple Cajun Chicken Legs

Servings: 1
Cooking Time: 8 Minutes

Ingredients:
- 8 Chicken Legs, boneless
- 2 tbsp Olive Oil
- 2 tbsp Cajun Seasoning

Directions:
1. Preheat your grill to medium-high.
2. Brush them with the olive oil, and then rub the legs with the seasoning.
3. When the green light is on, arrange the legs onto the bottom plate.
4. Lower the lid, and let the legs cook closed, for about 8 to 10 minutes.
5. Serve with the favorite side dish, Enjoy!

Nutrition Info: Calories 370 ;Total Fats 19.2g ;Carbs 0.5g ;Protein 35g ;Fiber: 0g

37. Peach Glazed Chicken Breasts

Servings: 4
Cooking Time: 10 Minutes

Ingredients:
- For Chicken:
- ¼ teaspoon ground cinnamon
- ¼ teaspoon ground nutmeg
- ¼ teaspoon ground cloves
- Salt, as required
- 4 (5-6-ounce) boneless skinless chicken breasts
- For Glaze:
- 1 peach, peeled and pitted
- 1 chipotle in adobo sauce
- 2 tablespoons fresh lemon juice

Directions:
1. In a bowl, place spices and salt and mix well.
2. Rub the chicken breasts with the spice mixture evenly.
3. For glaze: in a food processor, place peach, chipotle and lemon juice and pulse until pureed.
4. Transfer into a bowl and set aside.
5. Place the water tray in the bottom of George Foreman Grill .
6. Place about 2 cups of lukewarm water into the water tray.
7. Place the drip pan over water tray and then arrange the heating element.
8. Now, place the grilling pan over heating element.
9. Plugin the George Foreman Grill and press the 'Power' button to turn it on.
10. Then press 'Fan" button.
11. Set the temperature settings according to manufacturer's directions.
12. Cover the grill with lid and let it preheat.
13. After preheating, remove the lid and grease the grilling pan.
14. Place the chicken breasts over the grilling pan.
15. Cover with the lid and cook for about 8-10 minutes per side, brushing with the glaze after every 2 minutes.
16. Serve hot.

Nutrition Info: (Per Serving):Calories 287 ;Total Fat 10.7 g ;Saturated Fat 3 g ;Cholesterol 126 mg ;Sodium 163 mg ;Total Carbs 3.9 g ;Fiber 0.8 g ;Sugar 3.7 g ;Protein 41.5 g

38. Tequila Chicken

Servings: 3
Cooking Time: 7 Minutes

Ingredients:
- 1/2 cup gold tequila
- 1 cup lime juice
- 1/2 cup orange juice
- 1 tablespoon chili powder
- 1 tablespoon minced jalapeno pepper
- 1 tablespoon minced fresh garlic
- 2 teaspoons kosher salt
- 1 teaspoon black pepper
- 3 boneless chicken breasts

Directions:
1. Mix tequila, lime juice, orange juice, chili powder, jalapeno pepper, garlic, black pepper and salt in a bowl.
2. Add chicken breasts to the tequila marinade, cover and marinate for 1 hour.
3. Turn the "Selector" knob to the "Grill Panini" side.
4. Preheat the bottom grill of George Foreman Grill at 350 degrees F and the upper grill plate on medium heat.
5. Once it is preheated, open the lid and place the chicken breasts in the Griddler.
6. Close the griddler's lid and grill the chicken breasts for 7 minutes.
7. Serve warm.

Nutrition Info: (Per Serving): Calories 352 ;Total Fat 14 g ;Saturated Fat 2 g ;Cholesterol 65 mg ;Sodium 220 mg ;Total Carbs 15.8 g ;Fiber 0.2 g ;Sugar 1 g ;Protein 26 g

39. Teriyaki Chicken Thighs

Servings: 4
Cooking Time: 7 Minutes

Ingredients:
- 4 Chicken Thighs
- ½ cup Brown Sugar
- ½ cup Teriyaki Sauce
- 2 tbsp Rice Vinegar
- 1 thumb-sized piece of Ginger, minced
- ¼ cup Water
- 2 tsp minced Garlic
- 1 tbsp Cornstarch

Directions:
1. Place the sugar, teriyaki sauce, vinegar, ginger, water, and garlic, in a bowl.
2. Mix to combine well.
3. Transfer half of the mixture to a saucepan and set aside.
4. Add the chicken thighs to the bowl, and coat well.
5. Cover the bowl with wrap, and place in the fridge. Let sit for one hour.
6. Preheat your grill to medium.
7. In the meantime, place the saucepan over medium heat and add the cornstarch. Cook until thickened. Remove from heat and set aside.
8. Arrange the thighs onto the preheated bottom and close the lid.
9. Cook for 5 minutes, then open, brush the thickened sauce over, and cover again.
10. Cook for additional minute or two.
11. Serve and enjoy!

Nutrition Info: Calories 321 ;Total Fats 11g ;Carbs 28g ;Protein 31g ;Fiber: 1g

40. Chicken Drumsticks

Servings: 5
Cooking Time: 40 Minutes

Ingredients:
- 2 tablespoons avocado oil
- 1 tablespoon fresh lime juice
- 1 teaspoon red chili powder
- 1 teaspoon garlic powder
- Salt, as required
- 5 (8-ounce) chicken drumsticks

Directions:
1. In a mixing bowl, mix avocado oil, lime juice, chili powder and garlic powder and mix well.
2. Add the chicken drumsticks and coat with the marinade generously.
3. Cover the bowl and refrigerate to marinate for about 30-60 minutes.
4. Place the water tray in the bottom of George Foreman Grill .
5. Place about 2 cups of lukewarm water into the water tray.
6. Place the drip pan over water tray and then arrange the heating element.
7. Now, place the grilling pan over heating element.
8. Plugin the George Foreman Grill and press the 'Power' button to turn it on.
9. Then press 'Fan" button.
10. Set the temperature settings according to manufacturer's directions.
11. Cover the grill with lid and let it preheat.
12. After preheating, remove the lid and grease the grilling pan.
13. Place the chicken drumsticks over the grilling pan.
14. Cover with the lid and cook for about 30-40 minutes, flipping after every 5 minutes.
15. Serve hot.

Nutrition Info: (Per Serving):Calories 395 ;Total Fat 13.8 g ;Saturated Fat 3.6 g ;Cholesterol 200 mg ;Sodium 218 mg ;Total Carbs 1 g ;Fiber 0.5 g ;Sugar 0.2 g ;Protein 62.6 g

41. Thyme Duck Breasts

Servings: 2
Cooking Time: 16 Minutes

Ingredients:
- 2 shallots, sliced thinly
- 1 tablespoon fresh ginger, minced
- 2 tablespoons fresh thyme, chopped
- Salt and ground black pepper, as required
- 2 duck breasts

Directions:
1. In a large bowl, place the shallots, ginger, thyme, salt, and black pepper, and mix well.
2. Add the duck breasts and coat with marinade evenly.
3. Refrigerate to marinate for about 2-12 hours.
4. Place the water tray in the bottom of George Foreman Grill.
5. Place about 2 cups of lukewarm water into the water tray.
6. Place the drip pan over water tray and then arrange the heating element.
7. Now, place the grilling pan over heating element.
8. Plugin the George Foreman Grill and press the 'Power' button to turn it on.
9. Then press 'Fan" button.
10. Set the temperature settings according to manufacturer's directions.
11. Cover the grill with lid and let it preheat.
12. After preheating, remove the lid and grease the grilling pan, skin-side down.
13. Place the duck breast over the grilling pan.
14. Cover with the lid and cook for about 6-8 minutes per side.
15. Serve hot.

Nutrition Info: (Per Serving):Calories 337 ;Total Fat 10.1 g ;Saturated Fat 0 g ;Cholesterol 0 mg ;Sodium 80 mg ;Total Carbs 3.4 g ;Fiber 0 g ;Sugar 0.1 g ;Protein 55.5 g

42. Glazed Chicken Drumsticks

Servings: 12
Cooking Time: 25 Minutes

Ingredients:
- 1 (10-ounce) jar red jalapeño pepper jelly
- ¼ cup fresh lime juice
- 12 (6-ounce) chicken drumsticks
- Salt and ground black pepper, as required

Directions:
1. In a small saucepan, add jelly and lime juice over medium heat and cook for about 3-5 minutes or until melted.
2. Remove from the heat and set aside.
3. Sprinkle the chicken drumsticks with salt and black pepper.
4. Place the water tray in the bottom of George Foreman Grill.
5. Place about 2 cups of lukewarm water into the water tray.
6. Place the drip pan over water tray and then arrange the heating element.
7. Now, place the grilling pan over heating element.
8. Plugin the George Foreman Grill and press the 'Power' button to turn it on.
9. Then press 'Fan" button.
10. Set the temperature settings according to manufacturer's directions.
11. Cover the grill with lid and let it preheat.
12. After preheating, remove the lid and grease the grilling pan.
13. Place the chicken drumsticks over the grilling pan.
14. Cover with the lid and cook for about 15-20 minutes, flipping occasionally.
15. In the last 5 minutes of cooking, baste the chicken thighs with jelly mixture.
16. Serve hot.

Nutrition Info: (Per Serving):Calories 359 ;Total Fat 9.7 g ;Saturated Fat 2.6 g ;Cholesterol 150 mg ;Sodium 155 mg ;Total Carbs 17.1 g ;Fiber 0 g ;Sugar 11.4 g ;Protein 46.8 g

43. Lemon Grilled Chicken Thighs

Servings: 4
Cooking Time: 6 Minutes

Ingredients:
- Juice and zest of 2 lemons
- 2 sprigs fresh rosemary, chopped
- 2 sprigs fresh sage, chopped
- 2 garlic cloves, smashed and chopped
- 1/4 teaspoon crushed red pepper
- 4 chicken thighs, trimmed
- Kosher salt, to taste

Directions:
1. Rub the chicken thighs with salt, oil, red pepper, garlic, sage, rosemary, lemon zest and juice.
2. Place the chicken in a bowl, cover and marinate for 1 hour for marination.
3. Turn the "Selector" knob to the "Grill Panini" side.
4. Preheat the bottom grill of George Foreman Grill at 350 degrees F and the upper grill plate on medium heat.
5. Once it is preheated, open the lid and place 2 chicken thighs in the Griddler.
6. Close the griddler's lid and grill the chicken for 6 minutes.
7. Transfer them to a plate and grill the remaining thighs.
8. Serve warm.

Nutrition Info: (Per Serving): Calories 388 ;Total Fat 8 g ;Saturated Fat 1 g ;Cholesterol 153mg ;sodium 339 mg ;Total Carbs 8 g ;Fiber 1 g ;Sugar 2 g ;Protein 13 g

44. Grilled Chicken Breast

Servings: 2
Cooking Time: 12 Minutes

Ingredients:
- 3 tablespoons olive oil
- 5 fresh basil leaves, torn
- 1 clove garlic, sliced
- 2 chicken breasts, boneless, skinless
- Kosher salt and black pepper, to taste

Directions:
1. Rub the chicken breasts with black pepper, salt, garlic, basil leaves and olive oil.
2. Turn the "Selector" knob to the "Grill Panini" side.
3. Preheat the bottom grill of George Foreman Grill at 350 degrees F and the upper grill plate on medium heat.
4. Once it is preheated, open the lid and place the chicken breasts in the Griddler.
5. Close the griddler's lid and grill the skewers for 12 minutes.
6. Serve warm.

Nutrition Info: (Per Serving): Calories 453 ;Total Fat 2.4 g ;Saturated Fat 3 g ;Cholesterol 21 mg ;Sodium 216 mg ;Total Carbs 18 g ;Fiber 2.3 g ;Sugar 1.2 g ;Protein 23.2 g

FISH & SEAFOOD RECIPES

45. Orange-glazed Salmon

Servings: 4
Cooking Time: 8 Minutes

Ingredients:
- 4 Salmon Fillets
- ½ tsp Garlic Powder
- 1 tsp Paprika
- ¼ tsp Cayenne Pepper
- 1 ¾ tsp Salt
- 1 tbsp Brown Sugar
- ¼ tsp Black Pepper
- Glaze:
- 1 tsp Salt
- 2 tbsp Soy Sauce
- Juice of 1 Orange
- 4 tbsp Maple Syrup

Directions:
1. Preheat your grill to medium and coat with cooking spray.
2. In a small bowl, combine the spices together, and then massage the mixture into the fish.
3. Arrange the salmon onto the bottom plate and cook with the lid off.
4. In the meantime, place the glaze ingredients in a saucepan over medium heat.
5. Cook for a couple of minutes, until thickened.
6. Once the salmon has been cooking for 3 minutes, flip it over.
7. Cook for another 3 minutes.
8. Then, brush with the glaze, lower the lid, and cook for an additional minute.
9. Serve with preferred side dish. Enjoy!

Nutrition Info: Calories 250 ;Total Fats 19g ;Carbs 7g ;Protein 22g ;Fiber: 0g

46. Seasoned Tuna

Servings: 2
Cooking Time: 6 Minutes

Ingredients:
- 2 (6-ounce) yellowfin tuna steaks
- 2 tablespoons blackening seasoning
- Olive oil cooking spray

Directions:
1. Coat the tuna steaks with the blackening seasoning evenly.
2. Then spray tuna steaks with cooking spray.
3. Place the water tray in the bottom of George Foreman Grill.
4. Place about 2 cups of lukewarm water into the water tray.
5. Place the drip pan over water tray and then arrange the heating element.
6. Now, place the grilling pan over heating element.
7. Plugin the George Foreman Grill and press the 'Power' button to turn it on.
8. Then press 'Fan" button.
9. Set the temperature settings according to manufacturer's directions.
10. Cover the grill with lid and let it preheat.
11. After preheating, remove the lid and grease the grilling pan.
12. Place the tuna steaks over the grilling pan.
13. Cover with the lid and cook for about 2-3 minutes per side.
14. Serve hot.

Nutrition Info: (Per Serving):Calories 313 ;Total Fat 10.7 g ;Saturated Fat 2.2 g ;Cholesterol 83 mg ;Sodium 169 mg ;Total Carbs 0 g ;Fiber 0 g ;Sugar 0 g ;Protein 50.9 g

47. Lemon Pepper Salmon With Cherry Tomatoes And Asparagus

Servings: 4
Cooking Time: 5 Minutes

Ingredients:
- 4 Salmon Fillets
- 8 Cherry Tomatoes
- 12 Asparagus Spears
- 2 tbsp Olive Oil
- ½ tsp Garlic Powder
- 1 tsp Lemon Pepper
- ½ tsp Onion Powder
- Salt, to taste

Directions:
1. Preheat your grill to 375 degrees F and cut the tomatoes in half.
2. Brush the salmon, tomatoes, and sparagus with olive oil, and then sprinkle with the spices.
3. Arrange the salmon fillets, cherry tomatoes, and asparagus spears, onto the bottom plate.
4. Gently, lower the lid, and cook the fish and veggies for about 5-6 minutes, or until you reach your desired doneness (check at the 5th minute).
5. Serve and enjoy!

Nutrition Info: Calories 240 ;Total Fats 14g ;Carbs 3.5g ;Protein 24g ;Fiber: 1.4g

48. Lemon-garlic Salmon

Servings: 4
Cooking Time: 7 Minutes

Ingredients:
- 2 garlic cloves, minced
- 2 teaspoons lemon zest, grated
- 1/2 teaspoon salt
- 1/2 teaspoon fresh rosemary, minced
- 1/2 teaspoon black pepper
- 4 salmon fillets (6 oz.)

Directions:
1. Mix garlic with lemon zest, salt, rosemary and black pepper in a bowl
2. Leave this spice mixture for 15 minutes then rub it over the salmon with this mixture.
3. Turn the "Selector" knob to the "Grill Panini" side.
4. Preheat the bottom grill of George Foreman Grill at 350 degrees F and the upper grill plate on medium heat.
5. Once it is preheated, open the lid and place the salmon in the Griddler.
6. Close the griddler's lid and grill the salmon for 7 minutes.
7. Serve warm.

Nutrition Info: (Per Serving): Calories 246 ;Total Fat 7.4 g ;Saturated Fat 4.6 g ;Cholesterol 105 mg ;Sodium 353 mg ;Total Carbs 19.4 g ;Sugar 6.5 g ;Fiber 2.7 g ;Protein 37.2 g

49. The Easiest Pesto Shrimp

Servings: 2
Cooking Time: 5 Minutes

Ingredients:
- 1-pound Shrimp, tails and shells discarded
- ½ cup Pesto Sauce

Directions:
1. Place the cleaned shrimp in a bowl and add the pesto sauce to it.
2. Mix gently with your hands, until each shrimp is coated with the sauce. Let sit for about 15 minutes.
3. In the meantime, preheat your grill to 350 degrees F.
4. Open the grill and arrange the shrimp onto the bottom plate.
5. Cook with the lid off for about 2-3 minutes. Flip over and cook for an additional 2 minutes.
6. Serve as desired and enjoy!

Nutrition Info: Calories 470 ;Total Fats 28.5g ;Carbs 3g ;Protein 50g ;Fiber: 0g

50. Barbecue Squid

Servings: 4
Cooking Time: 3 Minutes

Ingredients:
- 1 ½ pounds skinless squid tubes, sliced
- ⅓ cup red bell pepper, chopped
- 13 fresh red Thai chiles, stemmed
- 6 garlic cloves, minced
- 3 shallots, chopped
- 1 (1-inch) piece fresh ginger, chopped
- 6 tablespoons sugar
- 2 tablespoons soy sauce
- 1 ½ teaspoons black pepper
- ¼ teaspoon salt

Directions:
1. Blend bell pepper, red chilies, shallots, sugar, soy sauce, black pepper and salt in a blender.
2. Transfer this marinade to a Ziplock bag and ad squid tubes.
3. Seal the bag and refrigerate for 1 hour for marination.
4. Turn the "Selector" knob to the "Grill Panini" side.
5. Preheat the bottom grill of George Foreman Grill at 350 degrees F and the upper grill plate on medium heat.
6. Once it is preheated, open the lid and place the squid chunks in the Griddler.
7. Close the griddler's lid and grill the squid for 2-3 minutes.
8. Serve warm.

Nutrition Info: (Per Serving): Calories 248 ;Total Fat 15.7 g ;Saturated Fat 2.7 g ;Cholesterol 75 mg ;Sodium 94 mg ;Total Carbs 31.4 g ;Fiber 0.4 g ;Sugar 3.1 g ;Protein 24.9 g

51. Herbed Salmon

Servings: 4
Cooking Time: 8 Minutes

Ingredients:
- 2 garlic cloves, minced
- 1 teaspoon dried oregano, crushed
- 1 teaspoon dried basil, crushed
- Salt and ground black pepper, as required
- ¼ cup olive oil
- 2 tablespoons fresh lemon juice
- 4 (4-ounce) salmon fillets

Directions:
1. In a large bowl, add all ingredients except for salmon and mix well.
2. Add the salmon and coat with marinade generously.
3. Cover and refrigerate to marinate for at least 1 hour.
4. Place the water tray in the bottom of George Foreman Grill.
5. Place about 2 cups of lukewarm water into the water tray.
6. Place the drip pan over water tray and then arrange the heating element.
7. Now, place the grilling pan over heating element.
8. Plugin the George Foreman Grill and press the 'Power' button to turn it on.
9. Then press 'Fan" button.
10. Set the temperature settings according to manufacturer's directions.
11. Cover the grill with lid and let it preheat.
12. After preheating, remove the lid and grease the grilling pan.
13. Place the salmon fillets over the grilling pan.
14. Cover with the lid and cook for about 4 minutes per side.
15. Serve hot.

Nutrition Info: (Per Serving):Calories 263 ;Total Fat 19.7 g ;Saturated Fat 2.9 g ;Cholesterol 50 mg ;Sodium 91 mg ;Total Carbs 0.9 g ;Fiber 0.2 g ;Sugar 0.2 g ;Protein 22.2 g

52. Ginger Salmon

Servings: 3
Cooking Time: 8 Minutes

Ingredients:
- Sauce:
- ¼ tablespoons rice vinegar
- 1 teaspoons sugar
- 1/8 teaspoon salt
- ¼ tablespoon lime zest, grated
- 1/8 cup lime juice
- ½ tablespoon olive oil
- 1/8 teaspoon ground coriander
- 1/8 teaspoon ground black pepper
- 1/8 cup cilantro, chopped
- ¼ tablespoon onion, chopped
- ½ teaspoon ginger root, minced
- 1 garlic clove, minced
- 1 small cucumber, peeled, chopped
- Salmon:
- 2 tablespoons gingerroot, minced
- ¼ tablespoon lime juice
- ¼ tablespoon olive oil
- Salt, to taste
- Black pepper, to taste
- 3 (6 oz.) salmon fillets

Directions:
1. Start by blending the cucumber with all the sauce ingredients in a blender until smooth.
2. Season and rub the salmon fillets with ginger, oil, salt, black pepper, lime juice.
3. Turn the "Selector" knob to the "Grill Panini" side.
4. Preheat the bottom grill of George Foreman Grill at 350 degrees F and the upper grill plate on medium heat.
5. Once it is preheated, open the lid and place the salmon fillets in the Griddler.
6. Close the griddler's lid and grill the salmon fillets for 8 minutes.
7. Serve warm with cucumber sauce.

Nutrition Info: (Per Serving): Calories 457 ;Total Fat 19.1 g ;Saturated Fat 11 g ;Cholesterol 262 mg ;Sodium 557 mg ;Total Carbs 18.9 g ;Sugar 1.2 g ;Fiber 1.7 g ;Protein 32.5 g

53. Pistachio Pesto Shrimp

Servings: 4
Cooking Time: 4 Minutes

Ingredients:
- ¾ cup fresh arugula
- ½ cup fresh parsley, minced
- 1/3 cup shelled pistachios
- 2 tablespoons lemon juice
- 1 garlic clove, peeled
- ¼ teaspoon lemon zest, grated
- ½ cup olive oil
- ¼ cup Parmesan cheese, shredded
- ¼ teaspoon salt
- 1/8 teaspoon pepper
- 1 ½ lbs. jumbo shrimp, peeled and deveined

Directions:
1. Start by blending the arugula, parsley, pistachios, lemon juice, garlic, lemon zest, and olive oil in a blender until smooth.
2. Stir in salt, black pepper, Parmesan cheese, and mix well.
3. Toss the shrimp with the prepared sauce in a bowl then cover to refrigerate for 30 minutes.
4. Thread these pesto shrimps on the wooden skewers.
5. Turn the "Selector" knob to the "Grill Panini" side.
6. Preheat the bottom grill of George Foreman Grill at 350 degrees F and the upper grill plate on medium heat.
7. Once it is preheated, open the lid and place the pesto skewers in the Griddler.
8. Close the griddler's lid and grill the shrimp skewers for 4 minutes.
9. Serve warm.

Nutrition Info: (Per Serving): Calories 293 ;Total Fat 16 g ;Saturated Fat 2.3 g ;Cholesterol 75 mg ;Sodium 386 mg ;Total Carbs 5.2 g ;Sugar 2.6 g ;Fiber 1.9 g ;Protein 34.2 g

54. Grilled Garlic Scallops

Servings: 4
Cooking Time: 4 Minutes

Ingredients:
- 1/4 cup olive oil
- Juice of 1 lemon
- 3 garlic cloves minced
- 1 tablespoon Italian seasoning
- Salt and black pepper, to taste
- 1-pound scallops

Directions:
1. Mix Italian seasoning, black pepper, salt, garlic cloves, lemon juice and olive oil in a bowl.
2. Toss in scallops, mix gently, cover and refrigerate for 30 minutes.
3. Turn the "Selector" knob to the "Griddle" side.
4. Preheat the bottom grill of George Foreman Grill at 350 degrees F.
5. Once it is preheated, open the lid and place the scallops in the Griddler.
6. Grill the scallop for 2 minutes flip and grill for 2 minutes.
7. Serve warm.

Nutrition Info: (Per Serving): Calories 351 ;Total Fat 4 g ;Saturated Fat 6.3 g ;Cholesterol 360 mg ;Sodium 236 mg ;Total Carbs 19.1 g ;Sugar 0.3 g ;Fiber 0.1 g ;Protein 36 g

55. Lemony Cod

Servings: 2
Cooking Time: 14 Minutes

Ingredients:
- 1 garlic cloves, minced
- ½ tablespoon fresh olive oil
- 1 tablespoon fresh lemon juice
- ½ teaspoon dried rosemary, crushed
- ¼ teaspoon paprika
- Salt and ground black pepper, as required
- 2 (6-ounce) skinless, boneless cod fillets

Directions:
1. In a large bowl, mix together all ingredients except cod fillets.
2. Add the cod fillets and coat with garlic mixture generously.
3. Place the water tray in the bottom of George Foreman Grill .
4. Place about 2 cups of lukewarm water into the water tray.
5. Place the drip pan over water tray and then arrange the heating element.
6. Now, place the grilling pan over heating element.
7. Plugin the George Foreman Grill and press the 'Power' button to turn it on.
8. Then press 'Fan" button.
9. Set the temperature settings according to manufacturer's directions.
10. Cover the grill with lid and let it preheat.
11. After preheating, remove the lid and grease the grilling pan.
12. Place the cod fillets over the grilling pan.
13. Cover with the lid and cook for about 6-7 minutes per side.
14. Serve hot.

Nutrition Info: (Per Serving):Calories 173 ;Total Fat 5.2 g ;Saturated Fat 0.6 g ;Cholesterol 84 mg ;Sodium 186 mg ;Total Carbs 1 g ;Fiber 0.3 g ;Sugar 0.2 g ;Protein 30.6 g

56. Lemony Salmon

Servings: 4
Cooking Time: 14 Minutes

Ingredients:
- 2 garlic cloves, minced
- 1 tablespoon fresh lemon zest, grated
- 2 tablespoons butter, melted
- 2 tablespoons fresh lemon juice
- Salt and ground black pepper, as required
- 4 (6-ounce) boneless, skinless salmon fillets

Directions:
1. In a bowl, place all ingredients (except salmon fillets) and mix well.
2. Add the salmon fillets and coat with garlic mixture generously.
3. Place the water tray in the bottom of George Foreman Grill .
4. Place about 2 cups of lukewarm water into the water tray.
5. Place the drip pan over water tray and then arrange the heating element.
6. Now, place the grilling pan over heating element.
7. Plugin the George Foreman Grill and press the 'Power' button to turn it on.
8. Then press 'Fan" button.
9. Set the temperature settings according to manufacturer's directions.
10. Cover the grill with lid and let it preheat.
11. After preheating, remove the lid and grease the grilling pan.
12. Place the salmon fillets over the grilling pan.
13. Cover with the lid and cook for about 6-7 minutes per side.
14. Serve immediately.

Nutrition Info: (Per Serving):Calories 281 ;Total Fat 16.3 g ;Saturated Fat 5.2 g ;Cholesterol 90 mg ;Sodium 157 mg ;Total Carbs 1 g ;Fiber 0.2 g ;Sugar 0.3 g ;Protein 33.3 g

BEEF, PORK & LAMB RECIPES

57. American Burger

Servings: 4
Cooking Time: 9 Minutes

Ingredients:
- 1/2 cup seasoned bread crumbs
- 1 large egg, lightly beaten
- 1/2 teaspoon salt
- 1/2 teaspoon pepper
- 1-lb. ground beef
- 1 tablespoon olive oil

Directions:
1. Take all the ingredients for a burger in a suitable bowl except the oil and the buns.
2. Mix them thoroughly together and make 4 of the ½ inch patties.
3. Brush these patties with olive oil.
4. Turn the "Selector" knob to the "Grill Panini" side.
5. Preheat the bottom grill of George Foreman Grill at 350 degrees F and the upper grill plate on medium heat.
6. Once it is preheated, open the lid and place the patties in the Griddler.
7. Close the griddler's lid and grill the patties for 7-9 minutes.
8. Serve warm.

Nutrition Info: (Per Serving): Calories 301 ;Total Fat 15.8 g ;Saturated Fat 2.7 g ;Cholesterol 75 mg ;Sodium 389 mg ;Total Carbs 11.7 g ;Fiber 0.3g ;Sugar 0.1 g ;Protein 28.2 g

58. Fajita Skewers

Servings: 6
Cooking Time: 7 Minutes

Ingredients:
- 1 lb. sirloin steak, cubed
- 1 bunch scallions, cut into large pieces
- 1 pack flour tortillas, cut into triangles
- 4 large bell peppers, cubed
- olive oil, for drizzling
- Salt to taste
- Black pepper to taste

Directions:
1. Thread the steak, tortillas, peppers, and scallions on the skewers.
2. Drizzle salt, black pepper, and olive oil over the skewers.
3. Turn the "Selector" knob to the "Grill Panini" side.
4. Preheat the bottom grill of George Foreman Grill at 350 degrees F and the upper grill plate on medium heat.
5. Once it is preheated, open the lid and place the fajita skewers in the Griddler.
6. Close the griddler's lid and grill the skewers for 7 minutes.
7. Serve warm.

Nutrition Info: (Per Serving): Calories 353 ;Total Fat 7.5 g ;Saturated Fat 1.1 g ;Cholesterol 20 mg ;Sodium 297 mg ;Total Carbs 10.4 g ;Fiber 0.2 g ;Sugar 0.1 g ;Protein 13.1 g

59. Garlicky Flank Steak

Servings: 6
Cooking Time: 15 Minutes

Ingredients:
- 3 garlic cloves, minced
- 2 tablespoons fresh rosemary, chopped
- Salt and ground black pepper, as required
- 2 pounds flank steak, trimmed

Directions:
1. In a large bowl, add all the ingredients except the steak and mix until well combined.
2. Add the steak and coat with the mixture generously.
3. Set aside for about 10 minutes.
4. Place the water tray in the bottom of George Foreman Grill .
5. Place about 2 cups of lukewarm water into the water tray.
6. Place the drip pan over water tray and then arrange the heating element.
7. Now, place the grilling pan over heating element.
8. Plugin the George Foreman Grill and press the 'Power' button to turn it on.
9. Then press 'Fan" button.
10. Set the temperature settings according to manufacturer's directions.
11. Cover the grill with lid and let it preheat.
12. After preheating, remove the lid and grease the grilling pan.
13. Place the steak over the grilling pan.
14. Cover with the lid and cook for about 12-15 minutes, flipping after every 3-4 minutes.
15. Remove from the grill and place the steak onto a cutting board for about 5 minutes.
16. With a sharp knife, cut the steak into desired sized slices and serve.

Nutrition Info: (Per Serving):Calories 299 ;Total Fat 12.8 g ;Saturated Fat 5.3 g ;Cholesterol 83 mg ;Sodium 113 mg ;Total Carbs 1.2 g ;Fiber 0.5 g ;Sugar 0 g ;Protein 42.2 g

60. Lamb Steak

Servings: 6
Cooking Time: 4 Minutes

Ingredients:
- 2 garlic cloves, minced
- 2 tablespoons olive oil
- 2 teaspoons dried oregano, crushed
- 2 tablespoons sumac
- 2 teaspoons sweet paprika
- 12 lamb cutlets, trimmed

Directions:
1. In a bowl mix together all ingredients except for lamb cutlets.
2. Add the cutlets and coat with garlic mixture evenly.
3. Set aside for at least 10 minutes.
4. Place the water tray in the bottom of George Foreman Grill.
5. Place about 2 cups of lukewarm water into the water tray.
6. Place the drip pan over water tray and then arrange the heating element.
7. Now, place the grilling pan over heating element.
8. Plugin the George Foreman Grill and press the 'Power' button to turn it on.
9. Then press 'Fan" button.
10. Set the temperature settings according to manufacturer's directions.
11. Cover the grill with lid and let it preheat.
12. After preheating, remove the lid and grease the grilling pan.
13. Place the cutlets over the grilling pan.
14. Cover with the lid and cook for about 2 minutes from both sides or until desired doneness.
15. Serve hot.

Nutrition Info: (Per Serving):Calories 343 ;Total Fat 16.6 g ;Saturated Fat 4.9 g ;Cholesterol 144 mg ;Sodium 122 mg ;Total Carbs 1 g ;Fiber 0.5 g ;Sugar 0.1 g ;Protein 45.2 g

61. Steak Skewers With Potatoes And Mushrooms

Servings: 6
Cooking Time: 10 Minutes

Ingredients:
- 1-pound Steak
- 4 tbsp Olive Oil
- ½ pound Button Mushrooms
- 4 tbsp Balsamic Vinegar
- 1 pound Very Small Potatoes, boiled
- 2 tsp minced Garlic
- ½ tsp dired Sage
- Salt and Pepper, to taste

Directions:
1. Start by cutting the steak into 1-inch pieces.
2. Quarter the mushrooms.
3. Whisk the vinegar, oil, garlic, sage, and salt and pepper, in a bowl.
4. Add the meat, murshooms and potatoes to the bowl, coat well, and place in the fridge for 30 minutes. If your potatoes are not small enough for the skewers, you can chop them into smaller chunks.
5. In the meantime, soak the skewers in cold water.
6. Meanwhile, preheat your grill to medium-high.
7. Thread the chunks onto the skewers and arrange them on the bottom plate.
8. Keep the lid open and cook for 5.
9. Flip over and cook for 5 more minutes.
10. Serve and enjoy!

Nutrition Info: Calories 383 ;Total Fats 23g ;Carbs 21g ;Protein 23g ;Fiber: 3g

62. Cheese Burgers

Servings: 4
Cooking Time: 8 Minutes

Ingredients:
- 1/2 cup cheddar cheese, shredded
- 6 tablespoons chili sauce
- 1 tablespoon chili powder
- 1-lb. ground beef

Directions:
1. First, take all the ingredients for patties in a bowl.
2. Thoroughly mix them together then make 4 of the ½ inch patties out of it.
3. Turn the "Selector" knob to the "Grill Panini" side.
4. Preheat the bottom grill of George Foreman Grill at 350 degrees F and the upper grill plate on medium heat.
5. Once it is preheated, open the lid and place the patties in the Griddler.
6. Close the griddler's lid and grill the patties for 8 minutes.
7. Serve warm.

Nutrition Info: (Per Serving): Calories 537 ;Total Fat 19.8 g ;Saturated Fat 1.4 g ;Cholesterol 10 mg ;Sodium 719 mg ;Total Carbs 15.1 g ;Fiber 0.9 g ;Sugar 1.4 g ;Protein 37.8 g

63. Grilled Lamb With Herbes De Provence

Servings: 6
Cooking Time: 18 Minutes

Ingredients:
- 1 rib (3 ounces-1-inch-thick) lamb chops
- 1/4 cups olive oil
- 2 lemons, juiced
- Salt and black pepper, to taste
- 3 tablespoons Herbes de Provence

Directions:
1. Rub the lamb chops with lemon juice, olive oil, black pepper, salt and Herbes de Provence.
2. Cover and marinate the chops for 1 hour in the refrigerator.
3. Turn the "Selector" knob to the "Grill Panini" side.
4. Preheat the bottom grill of George Foreman Grill at 350 degrees F and the upper grill plate on medium heat.
5. Once it is preheated, open the lid and place half of the chops in the Griddler.
6. Close the griddler's lid and grill the chops for 9 minutes.
7. Transfer the grilled chops to a plate and grill the remaining chops in the same manner.
8. Serve warm.

Nutrition Info: (Per Serving): Calories 308 ;Total Fat 20.5 g ;Saturated Fat 3 g ;Cholesterol 42 mg ;Sodium 688 mg ;Total Carbs 40.3 g ;Sugar 1.4 g ;Fiber 4.3 g ;Protein 49 g

64. Pork Kabobs

Servings: 6
Cooking Time: 10 Minutes

Ingredients:
- 1 tablespoon smoked paprika
- 1 teaspoon onion powder
- ½ teaspoon garlic powder
- ¼ teaspoon cayenne pepper
- Salt and ground black pepper, as required
- 2 (¾-pound) pork tenderloins, trimmed and cut into 1-inch cubes
- ¼ cup balsamic vinegar
- 3 tablespoons honey
- 1 tablespoon Dijon mustard
- 2 teaspoons olive oil
- 12 dried figs, halved

Directions:
1. In a bowl, mix together the spices, salt and black pepper.
2. Add pork cubes and coat with the spice mixture generously.
3. Cover the bowl and refrigerate for about 30 minutes.
4. For glaze: in a bowl, place vinegar, honey, mustard and oil and beat until well combined.
5. Thread the pork cubes and fig halves onto pre-soaked wooden skewers.
6. Place the water tray in the bottom of George Foreman Grill.
7. Place about 2 cups of lukewarm water into the water tray.
8. Place the drip pan over water tray and then arrange the heating element.
9. Now, place the grilling pan over heating element.
10. Plugin the George Foreman Grill and press the 'Power' button to turn it on.
11. Then press 'Fan" button.
12. Set the temperature settings according to manufacturer's directions.
13. Cover the grill with lid and let it preheat.
14. After preheating, remove the lid and grease the grilling pan.
15. Place the skewers over the grilling pan.
16. Cover with the lid and cook for about 8-10 minutes, flipping and basting with glaze occasionally.
17. Serve hot.

Nutrition Info: (Per Serving):Calories 377 ;Total Fat 11.4 g ;Saturated Fat 3.6 g ;Cholesterol 107 mg ;Sodium 135 mg ;Total Carbs 34.3 g ;Fiber 4.3 g ;Sugar 27.2 g ;Protein 35.5 g

65. Grilled Pork Chops

Servings: 4
Cooking Time: 20 Minutes

Ingredients:
- 4 pork chops bone in
- 1/4 cup olive oil
- 1 1/2 tablespoons brown sugar
- 2 teaspoons Dijon mustard
- 1 1/2 tablespoons soy sauce
- 1 teaspoon lemon zest
- 2 teaspoons parsley chopped
- 2 teaspoons thyme leaves, chopped
- 1/2 teaspoon salt
- 1/2 teaspoon black pepper
- 1 teaspoon garlic, minced

Directions:
1. Mix olive oil, brown sugar, Dijon mustard, soy sauce, lemon zest, parsley, thyme, salt, black pepper and garlic in a large and shallow bowl.
2. Add pork chops to the mixture and rub the spices all over.
3. Cover the pork chops and refrigerate for 1-8 hours for marination.
4. Turn the "Selector" knob to the "Grill Panini" side.
5. Preheat the bottom grill of George Foreman Grill at 350 degrees F and the upper grill plate on medium heat.
6. Once it is preheated, open the lid and place 2 pork chops in the Griddler.
7. Close the griddler's lid and grill the pork chops for 10 minutes.
8. Cook the rest of the chops in the same way.
9. Serve warm.

Nutrition Info: (Per Serving): Calories 545 ;Total Fat 36.4 g ;Saturated Fat 10.1 g ;Cholesterol 200 mg ;Sodium 272 mg ;Total Carbs 40.7 g ;Fiber 0.2 g ;Sugar 0.1 g ;Protein 42.5 g

66. Spiced Pork Tenderloin

Servings: 6
Cooking Time: 18 Minutes

Ingredients:
- 2 teaspoons fennel seeds
- 2 teaspoons coriander seeds
- 2 teaspoons caraway seeds
- 1 teaspoon cumin seeds
- 1 bay leaf
- Salt and freshly ground black pepper, to taste
- 2 tablespoons fresh dill, chopped
- 2 (1-pound) pork tenderloins, trimmed

Directions:
1. For spice rub: in a spice grinder, add the seeds and bay leaf and grind until finely powdered.
2. Add the salt and black pepper and mix.
3. In a small bowl, reserve 2 tablespoons of spice rub.
4. In another small bowl, mix together the remaining spice rub, and dill.
5. Place 1 tenderloin onto a piece of plastic wrap.
6. With a sharp knife, slice through the meat to within ½-inch of the opposite side. Now, open the tenderloin like a book.
7. Cover with another plastic wrap and with a meat pounder, gently pound into ½-inch thickness.
8. Repeat with the remaining tenderloin.
9. Remove the plastic wrap and spread half of the spice and dill mixture over the center of each tenderloin.
10. Roll each tenderloin like a cylinder.
11. With a kitchen string, tightly tie each roll at several places.
12. Rub each roll with the reserved spice rub generously.
13. With 1 plastic wrap, wrap each roll and refrigerate for at least 4-6 hours.
14. Place the water tray in the bottom of George Foreman Grill .
15. Place about 2 cups of lukewarm water into the water tray.
16. Place the drip pan over water tray and then arrange the heating element.
17. Now, place the grilling pan over heating element.
18. Plugin the George Foreman Grill and press the 'Power' button to turn it on.
19. Then press 'Fan" button.
20. Set the temperature settings according to manufacturer's directions.
21. Cover the grill with lid and let it preheat.
22. After preheating, remove the lid and grease the grilling pan.
23. Remove the plastic wrap from tenderloins.
24. Place the tenderloins over the grilling pan.
25. Cover with the lid and cook for about 14-18 minutes, flipping occasionally.
26. Remove from the grill and place tenderloins onto a cutting board.
27. With a piece of foil, cover each tenderloin for at least 5-10 minutes before slicing.
28. With a sharp knife, cut the tenderloins into desired size slices and serve.

Nutrition Info: (Per Serving):Calories 313 ;Total Fat 12.6 g ;Saturated Fat 4.4 g ;Cholesterol 142 mg ;Sodium 127 mg ;Total Carbs 1.4 g ;Fiber 0.7 g ;Sugar 0 g ;Protein 45.7 g

67. Maple Pork Chops

Servings: 1
Cooking Time: 7-8 Minutes

Ingredients:
- 4 boneless Pork Chops
- 6 tbsp Balsamic Vinegar
- 6 tbsp Maple Syrup
- ¼ tsp ground Sage
- Salt and Pepper, to taste

Directions:
1. Whisk the vinegar, maple, sage, and some salt and pepper in a bowl.
2. Add the pork chops and coat well.
3. Cover with plastic foil and refrigerate for one hour.
4. Preheat your grill to 350 degrees F.
5. Open and arrange the chops onto the bottom plate.
6. Lower the lid and cook closed for about 7 minutes, or until your desired doneness is reached.
7. Serve and enjoy!

Nutrition Info: Calories 509 ;Total Fats 19g ;Carbs 15g ;Protein 65g ;Fiber: 0g

68. Honey Glazed Pork Chops

Servings: 4
Cooking Time: 20 Minutes

Ingredients:
- 1/4 cup honey
- 1/2 cup low-sodium soy sauce
- 2 garlic cloves, minced
- Red pepper flakes, to taste
- 4 boneless pork chops

Directions:
1. Mix honey, soy sauce, garlic and red pepper flakes in a bowl.
2. Brush this honey mixture over the pork chops, liberally then marinate for 30 minutes.
3. Turn the "Selector" knob to the "Grill Panini" side.
4. Preheat the bottom grill of George Foreman Grill at 350 degrees F and the upper grill plate on medium heat.
5. Once it is preheated, open the lid and place 2 pork chops in the Griddler.
6. Close the griddler's lid and grill the chops for 10 minutes.
7. Transfer these chops to a plate and grill the remaining chops in the same manner.
8. Serve warm.

Nutrition Info: (Per Serving): Calories 695 ;Total Fat 17.5 g ;Saturated Fat 4.8 g ;Cholesterol 283 mg ;Sodium 355 mg ;Total Carbs 26.4 g ;Fiber 1.8 g ;Sugar 0.8 g ;Protein 47.4 g

BREADS AND SANDWICHES

69. The Greatest Butter Burger Recipe

Servings: 6
Cooking Time: 11 Minutes

Ingredients:
- 2 pounds Ground Chuck Meat
- 1 ½ tsp minced Garlic
- 6 tbsp Butter
- 2 tbsp Worcestershire Sauce
- 1 tsp Salt
- ½ tsp Pepper
- 6 Hamburger Buns
- Veggie Toppings of Choice

Directions:
1. Preheat your grill to medium-high.
2. Meanwhile, place the meat, garlic, sauce, salt, and pepper, in a bowl.
3. Mix with your hands to incorporate well. Make six patties out of the mixture.
4. Into each patty, press about one tablespoon into the center.
5. Open the grill and coat with some cooking spray.
6. Arrange the patties onto the bottom plate and cook for 6 minutes.
7. Flip over and cook for 5 more minutes.
8. Serve in hamburger buns with desired veggie toppings.
9. Enjoy!

Nutrition Info: Calories 595 ;Total Fats 48g ;Carbs 25g ;Protein 27g ;Fiber: 1.5g

70. Simple Pork Chop Sandwich

Servings: 4
Cooking Time: 7 Minutes

Ingredients:
- 4 Hamburger Buns
- 4 Cheddar Slices
- 4 boneless Pork Chop
- Salt and Pepper, to taste
- 4 tbsp Mayonnaise

Directions:
1. Preheat your grill to 375 degrees F.
2. When the green light turns on, open the grill.
3. Season the pork chops with salt and pepper and arrange onto the bottom plate.
4. Lower the lid, and cook the meat closed, for about 5-6 minutes.
5. Open the lid and place a slice of cheddar on top of each chop.
6. Cook for another minute or so, uncovered, until the cheese starts to melt.
7. Spread a tbsp of mayonnaise onto the insides of each bun.
8. Place the cheesy pork chop inside and serve.
9. Enjoy!

Nutrition Info: Calories 510 ;Total Fats 30.6g ;Carbs 18.4g ;Protein 42g ;Fiber: 5g

71. Chicken Pesto Grilled Sandwich

Servings: 2
Cooking Time: 4 Minutes

Ingredients:
- 4 Slices of Bread
- 1 ½ cups shredded Mozzarella Cheese
- ½ cup Pesto Sauce
- 2 cups cooked and shredded Chicken Meat
- 8 Sundried Tomatoes
- 1 ½ tbsp Butter

Directions:
1. Preheat your grill to medium-high.
2. Combine the pesto and chicken in a bowl.
3. Brush the outsides of the bread with the butter.
4. Divide the pesto/chicken filling between two bread slices.
5. Top with sundried tomatoes and mozzarella cheese.
6. Open the grill and carefully transfer the loaded slices of bread onto the top bottom.
7. Top with the remaining bread slices, carefully.
8. Lower the lid, pressing gently.
9. Let the sandwiches cook for about 3-4 minutes, or until the desired doneness is reached.
10. Serve and enjoy!

Nutrition Info: Calories 725 ;Total Fats 44.5g ;Carbs 32g ;Protein 51g ;Fiber: 7.5g

72. Fish Tacos With Slaw And Mango Salsa

Servings: 4
Cooking Time: 6 Minutes

Ingredients:
- 4 Tortillas
- 1-pound Cod
- 3 tbsp butter, melted
- ½ tsp Paprika
- ¼ tsp Garlic Onion
- 1 tsp Thyme
- ½ tsp Onion Powder
- ½ tsp Cayenne Pepper
- 1 tsp Brown Sugar
- 1 cup prepared (or store-brought) Slaw
- Salt and Pepper, to taste
- Mango Salsa:
- ¼ cup diced Red Onions
- Juice of 1 Lime
- 1 Mango, diced
- 1 Jalapeno Pepper, deseeded and minced
- 1 tbsp chopped Parlsey or Cilantro

Directions:
1. Preheat your grill to medium.
2. Brush the butter over the cod and sprinkle with the spices.
3. When ready, open the grill, and arrange the cod fillets onto the bottom plate.
4. Lower the lid and cook for about 4-5 minutes in total.
5. Transfer to a plate and cut into chunks.
6. Place all of the mango salsa ingredients in a bowl and mix to combine.
7. Assemble the tacos by adding slaw, topping with grilled cod, and adding a tablespoon or so of the mango salsa.
8. Enjoy!

Nutrition Info: Calories 323 ;Total Fats 12g ;Carbs 31g ;Protein 24g ;Fiber: 3g

73. Buttery Pepperoni Grilled Cheese Sandwich

Servings: 2
Cooking Time: 5 Minutes

Ingredients:
- 4 slices of Bread
- 4 slices of Mozzarella Cheese
- 4 tbsp Butter
- 18 Pepperoni Slices

Directions:
1. Preheat your grill to medium-high.
2. Meanwhile, brush each slice of bread with a tablespoon of butter. It seems like too much, but the taste is just incredible.
3. Divide the mozzarella and pepperoni among the insides of two bread slices.
4. Top the sandwich with the other slices of bread, keeping the buttery side up.
5. When the green light appears, open the grill.
6. Place the sandwiches carefully onto the bottom plate.
7. Lower the lid, and gently press.
8. Allow the sandwich to cook for 4-5 minutes.
9. Open the lid, transfer to a serving plate, cut in half, and serve. Enjoy!

Nutrition Info: Calories 625 ;Total Fats 46g ;Carbs 29g ;Protein 22g ;Fiber: 2g

74. Cheesy Buffalo Avocado Sandwich

Servings: 4
Cooking Time: 4 Minutes

Ingredients:
- 1 Avocado
- 2 Bread Slices
- 2 slices Cheddar Cheese
- 1 tbsp Butter
- Buffalo Sauce:
- 4 tbsp Hot Sauce
- 1 tbs White Vinegar
- ¼ cup Butter
- ¼ tsp Salt
- 1 tsp Cayenne Pepper
- ¼ tsp Garlic Salt

Directions:
1. Preheat your grill to 375 degrees F.
2. Meanwhile, peel the avocado, scoop out the flash, and mash it with a fork.
3. Spread the avocado onto a bread slice, and top with the cheddar cheese.
4. Spread the butter onto the outside of the other bread slice.
5. Top the sandwich with the buttery slice, with the butter-side up.
6. Grease the bottom cooking plate and place the sandwich there, with the butter-side up.
7. Lower the lid, press, and let the sandwich grill for about 4 minutes.
8. Meanwhile, whisk together all of the sauce ingredients.
9. Serve the sandwich with the Buffalo sauce and enjoy!

Nutrition Info: Calories 485 ;Total Fats 24g ;Carbs 35g ;Protein 8g ;Fiber: 3g

SNACK & DESSERT RECIPES

75. Rum-soaked Pineapple

Servings: 4
Cooking Time: 14 Minutes

Ingredients:
- 1/2 cup rum
- 1/2 cup packed brown sugar
- 1 teaspoon ground cinnamon
- 1 pineapple, cored and sliced
- Vanilla ice cream

Directions:
1. Mix run with cinnamon and brown sugar in a suitable bowl.
2. Pour this mixture over the pineapple rings and mix well.
3. Let them soak for 15 minutes and flip the pineapples after 7 minutes.
4. Turn the "Selector" knob to the "Grill Panini" side.
5. Preheat the bottom grill of George Foreman Grill at 350 degrees F and the upper grill plate on medium heat.
6. Once it is preheated, open the lid and place the pineapple slices in the Griddler.
7. Close the griddler's lid and grill the pineapple for 5-7 minutes until lightly charred.
8. Serve with ice cream.

Nutrition Info: (Per Serving): Calories 427 ;Total Fat 31.1 g ;Saturated Fat 4.2 g ;Cholesterol 123 mg ;Sodium 86 mg ;Total Carbs 49 g ;Sugar 12.4 g ;Fiber 19.8 g ;Protein 13.5 g

76. Fruit Kabobs

Servings: 6
Cooking Time: 9 Minutes

Ingredients:
- 1 tablespoon butter
- 1/2 cup apricot preserves
- 1 tablespoon water
- 1/8 teaspoon ground cinnamon
- 1/8 teaspoon ground nutmeg
- 3 nectarines, quartered
- 3 peaches, quartered
- 3 plums, quartered
- 1 loaf (10 ¾ oz.) lb. cake, cubed

Directions:
1. Take the first five ingredients in a small saucepan and stir cook for 3 minutes on medium heat.
2. Alternately thread the lb. cake and fruits on the skewers.
3. Brush these skewers with the apricot mixture.
4. Turn the "Selector" knob to the "Grill Panini" side.
5. Preheat the bottom grill of George Foreman Grill at 350 degrees F and the upper grill plate on medium heat.
6. Once it is preheated, open the lid and place the fruit skewers in the Griddler.
7. Close the griddler's lid and grill the skewers for 4-6 minutes until lightly charred.
8. Serve.

Nutrition Info: (Per Serving): Calories 248 ;Total Fat 15.7 g ;Saturated Fat 2.7 g ;Cholesterol 75 mg ;Sodium 94 mg ;Total Carbs 38.4 g ;Fiber 0.3 g ;Sugar 10.1 g ;Protein 14.1 g

77. Grilled Apples

Servings: 4
Cooking Time: 7 Minutes

Ingredients:
- 2 firm tart-sweet apples, sliced
- 2 tablespoons butter, melted
- 2 tablespoons brown sugar
- 2 tablespoons white sugar
- 1 teaspoon cinnamon
- 1/4 teaspoon ginger
- 1/4 teaspoon nutmeg

Directions:
1. Mix sugar with butter, ginger, nutmeg, and cinnamon in a bowl.
2. Turn the "Selector" knob to the "Grill Panini" side.
3. Preheat the bottom grill of George Foreman Grill at 350 degrees F and the upper grill plate on medium heat.
4. Once it is preheated, open the lid and place the apple slices in the Griddler.
5. Close the griddler's lid and grill the apples for 7 minutes.
6. Drizzle cinnamon butter on top and serve.

Nutrition Info: (Per Serving): Calories 319 ;Total Fat 11.9 g ;Saturated Fat 1.7 g ;Cholesterol 78 mg ;Sodium 79 mg ;Total Carbs 14.8 g ;Fiber 1.1 g ;Sugar 8.3 g ;Protein 5 g

78. Cinnamon Sugar Grilled Apricots

Servings: 4
Cooking Time: 6 Minutes

Ingredients:
- 6 smallish Apricots
- 1 tbsp Butter, melted
- 3 tbsp Brown Sugar
- ½ tbsp Cinnamon

Directions:
1. Preheat your grill to 350 degrees F.
2. Cut the apricots in half and discard the seeds.
3. When ready, open the grill and coat with cooking spray.
4. Arrange the apricots and cook for 3 minutes.
5. Flip over and cook for 3 minutes more.
6. Meanwhile, whisk together the butter, sugar, and cinnamon.
7. Transfer the grilled apricots to a serving plate.
8. Drizzle the sauce over.
9. Enjoy!

Nutrition Info: Calories 92 ;Total Fats 2g ;Carbs 17g ;Protein 1g ;Fiber: 1g

79. Banana Butter Kabobs

Servings: 6
Cooking Time: 3 Minutes

Ingredients:
- 1 loaf (10 ¾ oz.) cake, cubed
- 2 large bananas, one-inch slices
- 1/4 cup butter, melted
- 2 tablespoons brown sugar
- 1/2 teaspoon vanilla extract
- 1/8 teaspoon ground cinnamon
- 4 cups butter pecan ice cream
- 1/2 cup butterscotch ice cream topping
- 1/2 cup pecans, chopped and toasted

Directions:
1. Thread the cake and bananas over the skewers alternately.
2. Whisk butter with cinnamon, vanilla, and brown sugar in a small bowl.
3. Brush this mixture over the skewers liberally.
4. Turn the "Selector" knob to the "Grill Panini" side.
5. Preheat the bottom grill of George Foreman Grill at 300 degrees F and the upper grill plate on medium heat.
6. Once it is preheated, open the lid and place the banana skewers in the Griddler.
7. Close the griddler's lid and grill the skewers for 3 minutes.
8. Serve with ice cream, pecan, and butterscotch topping on top.

Nutrition Info: (Per Serving): Calories 419 ;Total Fat 19.7 g ;Saturated Fat 18.6 g ;Cholesterol 141 mg ;Sodium 193 mg ;Total Carbs 23.7 g ;Fiber 0.9 g ;Sugar 19.3 g ;Protein 5.2 g

80. Marshmallow Stuffed Banana

Servings: 1
Cooking Time: 8 Minutes

Ingredients:
- ¼ cup of chocolate chips
- 1 banana
- ¼ cup mini marshmallows

Directions:
1. Place a peeled banana over a 12 x 12-inch foil sheet.
2. Make a slit in the banana lengthwise and stuff this slit with chocolate chips and marshmallows.
3. Wrap the foil around the banana and seal it.
4. Turn the "Selector" knob to the "Griddle" side.
5. Prepare and preheat the bottom plate of George Foreman Grill at 300 degrees F.
6. Once it is preheated, open the lid and place the banana in the Griddler.
7. Cook the banana in the Griddler for 4 minutes, flip and cook for another 4 minutes.
8. Unwrap and serve.

Nutrition Info: (Per Serving): Calories 372 ;Total Fat 11.8 g ;Saturated Fat 4.4 g ;Cholesterol 62 mg ;Sodium 871 mg ;Total Carbs 45.8 g ;Fiber 0.6 g ;Sugar 27.3 g ;Protein 4 g

81. Peanut Butter Pancakes

Servings: 4
Cooking Time: 4 Minutes

Ingredients:
- 1 egg, beaten
- ½ cup Mozzarella cheese, shredded
- 3 tablespoons granulated Sugar
- 2 tablespoons peanut butter

Directions:
1. Turn the "Selector" knob to the "Griddle" side.
2. Preheat the bottom plate of the Cuisine GR Griddler at 350 degrees F.
3. In a medium bowl, put all ingredients and with a fork, mix until well combined.
4. Pour ¼ of the mixture into preheated Griddler and cook for about 2 minutes per side.
5. Cook for pancakes using the remaining batter.
6. Serve warm.

Nutrition Info: (Per Serving): Calories 145 ;Total Fat 11.5 g ;Saturated Fat 3.1 g ;Cholesterol 86 mg ;Sodium 147 mg ;Total Carbs 33.6 g ;Fiber 1 g ;Sugar 1.7 g ;Protein 8.8 g

82. Zucchini Rollups With Hummus

Servings: 4
Cooking Time: 3 Minutes

Ingredients:
- 2 medium Zucchini
- 6 tbsp Hummus
- 1 tbsp Olive Oil
- 1 Roasted Red Pepper, diced
- Salt and Pepper, to taste

Directions:
1. Preheat your grill to medium high.
2. Peel and slice the zucchini lengthwise.
3. Brush with olive oil and season with salt and pepper, generously.
4. Open the grill and arrange the zucchini slices on top.
5. Close the grill and cook for 2-3 minutes.
6. Transfer to a serving plate and let cool a bit until safe to handle.
7. Divide the hummus and red pepper among the grilled zucchini.
8. Roll up and secure the filling with a toothpick.
9. Serve and enjoy!

Nutrition Info: Calories 43 ;Total Fats 3.1g ;Carbs 3.6g ;Protein 1g ;Fiber: 1g

83. Coconut-coated Pineapple

Servings: 6
Cooking Time: 6 Minutes

Ingredients:
- 1 Pineapple
- 2 tbsp Honey
- 1 tbsp Coconut Cream
- 1/3 cup Shredded Coconut

Directions:
1. Preheat your grill to medium high.
2. Meanwhile, peel and slice the coconut.
3. Thread each slice onto a soaked skewer.
4. Open the grill and arrange the skewers on top of the bottom plate.
5. Cook for 3 minutes per side.
6. Meanwhile, whisk together the honey and coconut cream.
7. Brush the pineapple with the mixture.
8. Place the coconut in a shallow bowl.
9. Coat the brushed pineapple with the coconut, on all sides.
10. Serve and enjoy!

Nutrition Info: Calories 75 ;Total Fats 20g ;Carbs 20g ;Protein 0g ;Fiber: 1g

84. Red Velvet Pancakes

Servings: 2
Cooking Time: 4 Minutes

Ingredients:
- 2 tablespoons cacao powder
- 2 tablespoons Sugar
- 1 egg, beaten
- 2 drops super red food coloring
- ¼ teaspoon baking powder
- 1 tablespoon heavy whipping cream

Directions:
1. Turn the "Selector" knob to the "Griddle" side.
2. Preheat the bottom plate of the Cuisine GR Griddler at 350 degrees F.
3. In a medium bowl, put all ingredients and with a fork, mix until well combined.
4. Pour ½ of the mixture into preheated Griddler and cook for about 2 minutes per side.
5. Cook more pancakes using the remaining batter.
6. Serve warm.

Nutrition Info: (Per Serving): Calories 370 ;Total Fat 6 g ;Saturated Fat 3 g ;Cholesterol 92 mg ;Sodium 34 mg ;Total Carbs 33.2 g ;Fiber 1.5 g ;Sugar 0.2 g ;Protein 3.9 g

85. Fruity Skewers

Servings: 4
Cooking Time: 6 Minutes

Ingredients:
- 1 Pineapple, cut into chunks
- 12 Strawberries, halved
- 2 Mangos, cut into chunks
- ½ cup Orange Juice
- 2 tbsp Honey
- 1 tbsp Brown Sugar
- 1 tbsp Butter

Directions:
1. Preheat your grill to medium high.
2. Thread the fruit chunks onto soaked skewers.
3. Open the grill and place the skewers on the bottom grilling plate.
4. Cook for 3 minutes.
5. Flip over and cook for additional 3 minutes.
6. Meanwhile, combine the remaining ingredients in a small saucepan, and cook until slightly thickened.
7. Drizzle over the fruit skewers and serve. Enjoy!

Nutrition Info: Calories 180 ;Total Fats 4g ;Carbs 22g ;Protein 2g ;Fiber: 1g

86. Blueberry Waffles

Servings: 4
Cooking Time: 6 Minutes

Ingredients:
- ¼ cup all-purpose flour
- 1 teaspoon baking powder
- 2 tablespoons butter, melted
- 2 large eggs
- 2 ounces blueberry preserves
- ¼ cup powdered sugar
- 1½ teaspoons vanilla extract

Directions:
1. Turn the "Selector" knob to the "Grill Panini" side.
2. Fix a waffle plates in the cuisine gr Griddler, preheat it at 350 degrees F and preheat the upper plate on medium heat.
3. In a bowl, add the butter and eggs and beat until creamy.
4. Add the blueberry preserves, sugar, vanilla extract and salt and beat until well combined.
5. Add the flour and baking powder and beat until well combined.
6. Pour ¼ of the mixture into preheated Griddler, close the lid and cook for about 3 minutes.
7. Cook for waffle using the remaining batter.
8. Serve warm.

Nutrition Info: (Per Serving): Calories 215 ;Total Fat 8.5 g ;Saturated Fat 9.1 g ;Cholesterol 116 mg ;Sodium 131 mg ;Total Carbs 21.6 g ;Fiber 1.1 g ;Sugar 4.7 g ;Protein 3.8 g

OTHER FAVORITE RECIPES

87. Pork And Veggie Salad

Servings: 1
Cooking Time: 8 Minutes

Ingredients:
- ½ pound Pork Tenderloin
- 1 Lettuce Head
- 1 Tomato, chopped
- 1 Cucumber, chopped
- 1 can Beans, drained
- 1 Carrot, julienned
- 2 tbsp Olive Oil
- 2 tbsp Sour Cream
- 1 tsp Dijon Mustard
- 1 tsp Lemon Juice
- 1 tbsp Honey
- Salt and Pepper, to taste

Directions:
1. Preheat your grill to medium-high.
2. Cut the pork into strips and season with salt and pepper.
3. Coat the grill with cooking spray and arrange the pork onto the bottom plate.
4. Lower the lid so you can cut the cooking time in half and cook for 5 minutes.
5. When done, transfer to a cutting board.
6. If you want to, you can cut the pork into even smaller bite-sized pieces at this point.
7. Add the oil, lemon juice, mustard, honey, sour cream, and some salt and pepper, to a large bowl.
8. Mix well to combine and add the veggies.
9. Toss well to coat.
10. Top the salad with the grilled pork.
11. Enjoy!

Nutrition Info: Calories 240 ;Total Fats 18g ;Carbs 15g ;Protein 20g ;Fiber: 2g

88. Shrimp Salad With Sour Cream And Dijon

Servings: 4
Cooking Time: 6 Minutes

Ingredients:
- 1-pound Shrimp
- 1 Lettuce Head
- 1 cup Baby Spinach
- 1 Cucumber
- 1 Tomato
- 1 tbsp chopped Parsley
- ½ cup Sour Cream
- 2 tbsp Lemon Juice
- 1 tbsp Honey
- 1 tbsp Dijon Mustard
- 2 tbsp Olive Oil
- Salt and Pepper, to taste

Directions:
1. Preheat your grill to medium-high.
2. When the green light is on, grease with cooking spray.
3. Season the shrimp with salt and pepper and arrange onto the bottom plate.
4. Cook for 2-3 minutes, then flip over, and cook for 2-3 minutes more.
5. Meanwhile, chop the veggies and place in a large bowl.
6. When ready, transfer the shrimp to the bowl.
7. In another bowl, whisk together the remaining ingredients.
8. Drizzle the sour cream mixture over the salad.
9. Serve and enjoy!

Nutrition Info: Calories 245 ;Total Fats 16g ;Carbs 12g ;Protein 20g ;Fiber: 2.2g

89. Lamb Burgers

Servings: 5
Cooking Time: 16 Minutes

Ingredients:
- 2 pounds ground lamb
- 9 ounces Halloumi cheese, grated
- 2 eggs
- 1 tablespoon fresh rosemary, chopped finely
- 1 tablespoon fresh parsley, chopped finely
- 2 teaspoons ground cumin
- Salt and ground black pepper, as required

Directions:
1. In a large bowl, add all the ingredients and mix until well combined.
2. Make 10 equal-sized patties from the mixture.
3. Place the water tray in the bottom of George Foreman Grill.
4. Place about 2 cups of lukewarm water into the water tray.
5. Place the drip pan over water tray and then arrange the heating element.
6. Now, place the grilling pan over heating element.
7. Plugin the George Foreman Grill and press the 'Power' button to turn it on.
8. Then press 'Fan" button.
9. Set the temperature settings according to manufacturer's directions.
10. Cover the grill with lid and let it preheat.
11. After preheating, remove the lid and grease the grilling pan.
12. Place the burgers over the grilling pan.
13. Cover with the lid and cook for about 15-8 minutes per side.
14. Serve hot

Nutrition Info: (Per Serving):Calories 554 ;Total Fat 30.6 g ;Saturated Fat 15.9 g ;Cholesterol 269 mg ;Sodium 459 mg ;Total Carbs 2.3 g ;Fiber 0.4 g ;Sugar 1.5 g ;Protein 64.4 g

90. Scrambled Eggs And Cheese

Servings: 2
Cooking Time: 5 Minutes

Ingredients:
- 2 large eggs
- 2 tablespoons milk
- 1/8 teaspoon cayenne pepper
- 1/4 teaspoon salt
- 1 scallion, thinly sliced
- 2 tablespoons cheddar cheese, shredded
- 1 cherry tomato, quartered

Directions:
1. Beat eggs with milk, cayenne pepper, salt, scallion, cheddar, and tomato in a bowl.
2. Open the top lid of the George Foreman Grill and set the flat plate sides up.
3. Turn the "Selector" knob to the "Grill Panini" side.
4. Preheat the bottom plate of George Foreman Grill at 350 degrees F and the upper plate on medium heat.
5. Once it is preheated, pour the egg mixture on both plates.
6. Stir and cook the eggs for 5 minutes until set.
7. Serve warm.

Nutrition Info: (Per Serving): Calories 117 ;Total Fat 7.7g ;Saturated Fat 3.2g ;Cholesterol 195mg ;Sodium 413mg ;Total Carbs 2.9g ;Fiber 0.6g ;Sugars 2.3g ;Protein 8.7g

91. Chocolate Panini

Servings: 4
Cooking Time: 5 Minutes

Ingredients:
- 4 challah bread slices
- 2 ounces semisweet chocolate, chopped

Directions:
1. Place the 2 bread slices on the working surface and top the bread with chocolate.
2. Set the remaining bread slices on top and press gently.
3. Cut the sandwiches into half diagonally.
4. Turn the "Selector" knob to the "Grill Panini" side.
5. Preheat the bottom grill of George Foreman Grill at 350 degrees F and the upper grill on medium heat.
6. Once it is preheated, place the sandwiches in the grill.
7. Close the griddler's lid and grill the panini for 5 minutes.
8. Serve warm.

Nutrition Info: (Per Serving): Calories 281 ;Total Fat 10.9g ;Saturated Fat 5.4g ;Cholesterol 0mg ;Sodium 327mg ;Total Carbs 44.1g ;Fiber 3.8g ;Sugars 19.9g ;Protein 5.7g

92. Beef Burgers

Servings: 4
Cooking Time: 8 Minutes

Ingredients:
- 1 pound lean ground beef
- ¼ cup fresh parsley, chopped
- ¼ cup fresh parsley, chopped
- ¼ cup fresh cilantro, chopped
- 1 tablespoon fresh ginger, chopped
- 1 teaspoon ground cumin
- 1 teaspoon ground coriander
- ½ teaspoon ground cinnamon
- Salt and ground black pepper, as required

Directions:
1. In a bowl, add the beef, ¼ cup of parsley, cilantro, ginger, spices, salt and black pepper and mix until well combined.
2. Make 4 equal-sized patties from the mixture.
3. Place the water tray in the bottom of George Foreman Grill .
4. Place about 2 cups of lukewarm water into the water tray.
5. Place the drip pan over water tray and then arrange the heating element.
6. Now, place the grilling pan over heating element.
7. Plugin the George Foreman Grill and press the 'Power' button to turn it on.
8. Then press 'Fan" button.
9. Set the temperature settings according to manufacturer's directions.
10. Cover the grill with lid and let it preheat.
11. After preheating, remove the lid and grease the grilling pan.
12. Place the burgers over the grilling pan.
13. Cover with the lid and cook for about for about 3-4 minutes per side or until desired doneness.
14. Serve hot.

Nutrition Info: (Per Serving):Calories 220 ;Total Fat 7.3 g ;Saturated Fat 2.7 g ;Cholesterol 101 mg ;Sodium 117 mg ;Total Carbs 1.7 g ;Fiber 0.5 g ;Sugar 0.1 g ;Protein 34.8 g

93. Turkey Burgers

Servings: 4
Cooking Time: 12 Minutes

Ingredients:
- Olive oil cooking spray
- 12 ounces lean ground turkey
- ½ of apple, peeled, cored and grated
- ½ of red bell pepper, seeded and chopped finely
- ¼ cup red onion, minced
- 2 small garlic cloves, minced
- 1 tablespoon fresh ginger, minced
- 2½ tablespoons fresh cilantro, chopped
- 2 tablespoons curry paste
- 1 teaspoon ground cumin
- 1 teaspoon olive oil

Directions:
1. In a large bowl, add all the ingredients except for oil and mix until well combined.
2. Make 4 equal-sized burgers from mixture.
3. Brush the burgers with olive oil evenly.
4. Place the water tray in the bottom of George Foreman Grill .
5. Place about 2 cups of lukewarm water into the water tray.
6. Place the drip pan over water tray and then arrange the heating element.
7. Now, place the grilling pan over heating element.
8. Plugin the George Foreman Grill and press the 'Power' button to turn it on.
9. Then press 'Fan" button.
10. Set the temperature settings according to manufacturer's directions.
11. Cover the grill with lid and let it preheat.
12. After preheating, remove the lid and grease the grilling pan.
13. Place the steak over the grilling pan.
14. Cover with the lid and cook for about 5-6 minutes per side.
15. Serve hot.

Nutrition Info: (Per Serving):Calories 258 ;Total Fat 15.2 g ;Saturated Fat 1.8 g ;Cholesterol 87 mg ;Sodium 94 mg ;Total Carbs 9.5 g ;Fiber 1.3 g ;Sugar 4 g ;Protein 24.3 g

94. Breakfast Panini

Servings: 2
Cooking Time: 5 Minutes

Ingredients:
- 3 teaspoons butter
- 1 scrambled egg
- 2 slices Italian sandwich bread
- 1 (3/4-ounce) slice Deli American
- 2 (1-ounce) slices ham

Directions:
1. Brush the top of one bread slice with butter.
2. Add scrambled egg, deli American and ham slices on top.
3. Place another bread slice on top.
4. Cut the sandwiches into half diagonally and brush the top with butter.
5. Turn the "Selector" knob to the "Grill Panini" side.
6. Preheat the bottom grill of George Foreman Grill at 350 degrees F and the upper grill on medium heat.
7. Once it is preheated, place the sandwiches in the grill.
8. Close the griddler's lid and grill the panini for 5 minutes.
9. Serve warm.

Nutrition Info: (Per Serving): Calories 233 ;Total Fat 16.1g ;Saturated Fat 7.4g ;Cholesterol 235mg ;Sodium 676mg ;Total Carbs 7.5g ;Fiber 0.6g ;Sugars 0.9g ;Protein 13.8g

95. Grilled Watermelon Salad With Cucumber And Cheese

Servings: 4
Cooking Time: 4 Minutes

Ingredients:
- 1 Small Watermelon (approximately yielding 4 cups when cubed)
- 1 tbsp chopped Basil
- 1 Cucumber, chopped
- 3 ounces Feta Cheese, crumbled or cubed
- Juice of 1 Lime
- 1 tbsp Olive Oil
- Salt and Pepper, to taste

Directions:
1. Preheat your grill to medium.
2. Peel and slice the watermelon (discard any seeds).
3. Open the grill and arrange the watermelon onto the bottom plate.
4. Lower the lid and cook for 4 minutes.
5. Transfer to a cutting board and slice into chunks.
6. Place into a bowl and add the rest of the ingredients.
7. Toss well to combine and coat.
8. Serve and enjoy!

Nutrition Info: Calories 122 ;Total Fats 5g ;Carbs 17g ;Protein 4g ;Fiber: 1g

96. Stuffed Burgers

Servings: 10
Cooking Time: 20 Minutes
Ingredients:
- For Filling:
- 2 cups cooked ham, chopped
- 2 cups fresh mushrooms, chopped
- 2 cups onion, chopped
- 3 cups cheddar cheese, shredded
- For Patties:
- 5 pounds lean ground beef
- 1/3 cup Worcestershire sauce
- 2 teaspoons hickory seasoning
- Salt and ground black pepper, as required

Directions:
1. For filling: in a bowl, mix together all ingredients. Set aside.
2. For patties: in another large bowl, add all ingredients and mix until well combined.
3. Divide beef mixture into 20 equal portions. Make equal sized patties from each portion.
4. Place 10 patties onto a smooth surface. Place cheese mixture over each patty evenly.
5. Cover with remaining patties, by pressing the edges to secure the filling.
6. Place the water tray in the bottom of George Foreman Grill .
7. Place about 2 cups of lukewarm water into the water tray.
8. Place the drip pan over water tray and then arrange the heating element.
9. Now, place the grilling pan over heating element.
10. Plugin the George Foreman Grill and press the 'Power' button to turn it on.
11. Then press 'Fan" button.
12. Set the temperature settings according to manufacturer's directions.
13. Cover the grill with lid and let it preheat.
14. After preheating, remove the lid and grease the grilling pan.
15. Place the burgers over the grilling pan.
16. Cover with the lid and cook for about 8-10 minutes per side.
17. Serve hot.

Nutrition Info: (Per Serving):Calories 623 ;Total Fat 27.7 g ;Saturated Fat 13.3 g ;Cholesterol 254 mg ;Sodium 865 mg ;Total Carbs 5.9 g ;Fiber 1 g ;Sugar 3.1 g ;Protein 82.4 g

97. Sausage Scrambled Eggs

Servings: 3
Cooking Time: 5 Minutes

Ingredients:
- 3 eggs
- ¼ cup milk
- Black pepper, to taste
- 2 ounces bulk pork sausage
- 2 bacon slices, chopped
- ¼ cup cooked ham, diced

Directions:
1. Beat eggs with milk, black pepper, pork sausage, and bacon in a bowl.
2. Open the top lid of the George Foreman Grill and set the flat plate sides up.
3. Turn the "Selector" knob to the "Grill Panini" side.
4. Preheat the bottom plate of George Foreman Grill at 350 degrees F and the upper plate on medium heat.
5. Once it is preheated, pour the egg mixture on both plates.
6. Stir and cook the eggs for 5 minutes until set.
7. Serve warm.

Nutrition Info: (Per Serving): Calories 224 ;Total Fat 16.4g ;Saturated Fat 5.4g ;Cholesterol 202mg ;Sodium 652mg ;Total Carbs 2g ;Fiber 0.2g ;Sugars 1.3g ;Protein 16.4g

98. Grilled Zucchini And Feta Salad

Servings: 4
Cooking Time: 3 Minutes

Ingredients:
- 1 Large Zucchini
- 1 cup Baby Spinach
- ½ cup crumbled Feta Cheese
- 1 cup Cherry Tomatoes, cut in half
- 1 cup Corn
- 3 tbsp Olive Oil
- 1 tsp Lemon Juice
- Salt and Pepper, to taste

Directions:
1. Preheat your grill to 350 degrees F.
2. Peel the zucchini and slice lengthwise. Season with salt and pepper.
3. Open the grill and coat with cooking spray.
4. Arrange the zucchini on top of the bottom plate and lower the lid.
5. Cook for 2-3 minutes.
6. Meanwhile, combine the remaining ingredients in a large bowl.
7. Transfer the zucchini to cutting bord and chop into pieces.
8. Add to the bowl and toss well to combine.
9. Serve and enjoy!

Nutrition Info: Calories 192 ;Total Fats 14.6g ;Carbs 12.6g ;Protein 5g ;Fiber: 2.7g

99. Mexican Scrambled Eggs

Servings: 4
Cooking Time: 5 Minutes

Ingredients:
- 2 tablespoons vegetable oil
- 1 tomato, roughly chopped
- 1 spring onion, chopped
- 1 green chili, chopped
- 4 large eggs, beaten
- ¼ teaspoon Maldon salt

Directions:
1. Beat eggs with vegetable oil, tomato, spring onion, green chili, and Maldon salt in a bowl.
2. Open the top lid of the George Foreman Grill and set the flat plate sides up.
3. Turn the "Selector" knob to the "Grill Panini" side.
4. Preheat the bottom plate of George Foreman Grill at 350 degrees F and the upper plate on medium heat.
5. Once it is preheated, pour the egg mixture on both plates.
6. Stir and cook the eggs for 5 minutes until set.
7. Serve warm.

Nutrition Info: (Per Serving): Calories 138 ;Total Fat 11.8g ;Saturated Fat 2.9g ;Cholesterol 186mg ;Sodium 101mg ;Total Carbs 1.8g ;Fiber 0.3g ;Sugars 1.1g ;Protein 6.5g

100. Greek Grilled Salmon Salad

Servings: 4
Cooking Time: 8 Minutes

Ingredients:
- 1-pound Salmon Fillets
- 4 cups chopped Lettuce
- 1 Red Onion, sliced
- 1/3 cup Kalamata Olives, pitted
- 1 Cucumber, chopped
- 1 Avocado, sliced
- 2 Tomatoes, chopped
- ½ cup Feta Cheese, crumbled
- 3 tbsp Olive Oil
- 1 tsp Oregano
- 1 tsp Basil
- 2 tbsp Lemon Juice
- Salt and Pepper, to taste

Directions:
1. Preheat your grill to medium-high.
2. When ready, open the grill and coat with cooking spray.
3. Season the salmon with salt and pepper and arrange onto the bottom plate.
4. Grill open, for about 4 minutes. Flip over, and grill for another 3 to 4 minutes.
5. Transfer to a cutting board and slice.
6. Place the veggies in a large bowl and toss to combine well.
7. Top the salad with the grilled salmon slices and feta cheese.
8. In a smaller bowl, whisk together the olive oil, lemon juice, oregano, basil, and some salt and pepper. Drizzel over the salad.
9. Serve and enjoy!

Nutrition Info: Calories 411 ;Total Fats 27g ;Carbs 12g ;Protein 28g ;Fiber: 6g

CPSIA information can be obtained
at www.ICGtesting.com
Printed in the USA
LVHW102332210221
679511LV00004B/346